D0907091

CULTURE COUNTS

Culture Counts

*Faith and Feeling
in a World Besieged*

ROGER SCRUTON

BRIEF ENCOUNTERS

Encounter Books · New York

First edition published in 2007 by Encounter Books, an activity of Encounter for Culture and Education, Inc., a nonprofit, tax exempt corporation.

Encounter Books website address: *www.encounterbooks.com*

Manufactured in the United States and printed on acid-free paper. The paper used in this publication meets the minimum requirements of ANSI/NISO Z39.48–1992 (R 1997) (Permanence of Paper).

FIRST EDITION

LIBRARY OF CONGRESS CATALOGING-IN-PUBLICATION DATA

Scruton, Roger.
Culture counts : faith and feeling in a world besieged / Roger Scruton.
  p. cm.
Includes bibliographical references.
ISBN-13: 978-1-59403-194-6 (hardcover : alk. paper)
ISBN-10: 1-59403-194-0 (hardcover)
1. Christianity and culture. I. Title.
BR115.C8S33 2007
909'.09821—dc22
2006039025

10 9 8 7 6 5 4 3 2

Contents

Preface

CHALLENGED FROM OUTSIDE by radical Islam and from within by "multiculturalism," Western societies are experiencing an acute crisis of identity. By what right do they exist, and by what achievement should they define themselves? In the nineteenth century they might have framed their answer in Christian terms. But most Westerners today —Christians included—hesitate to stress the religion that was once the primary source of their moral norms. Christianity has more the character of an intimate memory than a conquering gospel, and those who raise the cross in public are now subject to disheartening sarcasm and even open contempt. When Oswald Spengler published *The Decline of the West* in 1921, he saw Christianity as the heart of Western culture. But he argued that our once rich and living culture had been replaced by the lifeless precepts of a mere "civilization." When culture gives way to civilization, Spengler argued, we enter an age of decline.

There is much to deplore but also much to admire in Spengler,[1] and no one can doubt that the thesis of his book has gained in plausibility since he first announced it. At the same time, his vision, like that of Marx, is deeply parochial, fixed on the events that made the European continent great, and ignoring those that made it small—smaller by far than the Western civilization which Spengler claimed to be

Preface

discussing. For Spengler, the great event that brought Western culture to an end and launched it on the path of civilization was the French Revolution—the very same one whose
image of turmoil had fascinated Marx. The American Revolution, which preceded the French and which inaugurated
two hundred years of increasingly stable government, is not
even noticed in *The Decline of the West.* This event was not
drastic enough for Spengler, who was uninterested in the
normal flow of human happiness. As a result he overlooked
the event which led to the creation of the modern world: the
transformation of the European rule of law into a constitu-
tional democracy, implanted in a land that was both free
from history and isolated from the social norms of the European city. Here was a triumph that was to fascinate the world
and, in our own time, to inspire a bitter and destructive envy.

It is because of America, its success, its conflicts, and its
symbolic importance in the world, that the question raised
by Spengler is still with us: the question of Western identity.
Take away America, its freedom, its optimism, its institutions, its Judeo-Christian beliefs, and its educational tradition,
and little would remain of the West, besides the geriatric
routines of a now toothless Europe. Add America to the discussion, and all the dire prophecies and mournful valedic-
tions of the twentieth century seem faintly ridiculous. Yet,
precisely because the West now depends upon America, a
country launched on a path that recognizes no place and no
time as its own, Western identity has become an urgent
matter of debate. In referring to Western civilization we are
not, like Spengler, describing some localized and time-bound
fragment of human history. We are describing a project,
which grew from great events in the Mediterranean basin

two millennia ago, and which now engages the aspirations and the antipathies of all mankind. This project can endure, it seems to me, only if it can win a place in our emotions. The American experiment has placed two great gifts at the feet of mankind: viable democracy and masterful technology. But those benefits, which attract our praise and our pride, do not conquer the heart. They do not, in themselves, create the deep attachment on which the future of our civilization depends. They provide no outlook on human life and its meaning that can stand up either to the sarcastic nihilism of the West's internal critics or to the humorless bigotry of Islam. In the face of such enemies we need to affirm not our achievements, but *our right to exist*. Christianity enabled us to do this, by providing a vision of God's grace and our salvation. And so long as our civilization endures that vision will have force for us. But it is no longer a militant vision. Such strength as it has derives from the shared meanings conveyed to us by our culture— meanings conveyed equally to the one who believes and the one who doubts. For that very reason, however, culture has begun to have a new importance for us, as the repository of a threatened store of moral knowledge. Perhaps one day our culture will no longer be taught. If that happens, then the ideals and attachments that have come down to us will disappear, and our civilization will stand unprotected against the rising flood of the world's resentment.

Such, at least, is my belief. But you don't have to share that belief in order to follow the argument of this book. In it I defend what is sometimes called the "high culture" of Western civilization, by which I mean the literary, artistic, and philosophical inheritance that has been taught in departments of humanities both in Europe and in America, and which has recently been subject to contemptuous dismissal (especially in America) as the product of "dead white European males." I offer a definition of culture, and rebut the suggestion that cultures cannot be judged, either from inside or from outside, by objective standards. I argue that a culture is in a certain sense *composed* of judgments, and exists so as to pass on the habit of judgment from generation to generation. This habit of judgment is vital to moral development, and is the foundation of the rites of passage whereby young people leave the state of adolescence and undertake the burdens of adult life. A healthy society therefore requires a healthy culture, and this is so, even if culture, as I define it, is the possession not of the many but of the few.

Unlike science, culture is not a repository of factual information or theoretical truth, nor is it a kind of training in skills, whether rhetorical or practical. Yet it is a source of knowledge: *emotional* knowledge, concerning what to do and what to feel. We transmit this knowledge through ideals and examples, through images, narratives, and symbols. We transmit it through the forms and rhythms of music, and through the orders and patterns of our built environment. Such cultural expressions come about as a response to the perceived fragility of human life, and embody a collective recognition that we depend on things outside our control. Every culture therefore has its root in religion, and from this root the sap of moral knowledge spreads through all the branches of speculation and art. Our civilization has been uprooted. But when a tree is uprooted it does not always die. Sap may find its way to the branches, which break into leaf each spring with the perennial hope of living things. Such is our condition, and it is for this reason that culture has become not just precious to us, but a genuine political cause, the primary way of conserving our moral heritage and of standing firm in the face of a clouded future.

At the same time, the decline in religious faith means that many people, both skeptics and vacillators, begin to repudiate their cultural inheritance. The burden of this inheritance, without the consolations on offer to the believer, becomes intolerable, and creates the motive to scoff at those who seek to hand it on. Our educational institutions offer privileged positions to those who disparage the old values, old hierarchies and old forms of social order that lie hidden in the curriculum that has come down to us. There is nothing to teach in the name of culture, they tell us, except the prejudices of other ages. And they support this position with a variety of arguments, seized from the armory of philosophical skepticism, and put forward in proof of the view that there is no objective procedure, no authority, no secure canon of classics that would entitle us to judge one cultural product as superior to another. In the field of culture, they argue, anything goes, and also nothing.

Paradoxically, this new relativism, which has invaded every area of the humanities, goes hand in hand with an equally obstinate censoriousness. Many teachers are angry at the traditional works of our culture, and seek either to remove them from the curriculum or to hedge them around with prohibitions, seeing them as mere survivals of patriarchal, aristocratic, bourgeois, or theocratic attitudes that no longer have a claim on us. This posture of skepticism towards the classics displays a profound misjudgment. For the great works of Western culture are remarkable for the distance that they maintained from the norms and orthodoxies that gave birth to them. Only a very shallow reading of Chaucer or Shakespeare would see those writers as endorsing the societies in which they lived, or would overlook the far more important fact that their works hold mankind to the light of moral judgment, and examine, with all the love and all the pity that it calls for, the frailty of human nature. It is precisely the aspiration towards universal truth, towards a God's-eye perspective on the human condition, that is the hallmark of Western culture. And it is for that reason that we should see the American Revolution, rather than the French, as the turning point in our history, the moment when Western civilization became identical with the modern world—for that was the moment when Enlightenment took power.

The new curriculum in the humanities, which is relativist in favor of transgression and absolutist against authority, is one of the most striking phenomena of the modern university, and in this book I do my best to explain it. It presents an obstacle to cultural renewal and a challenge to those, like myself, who hope to indicate some methods of objective study that will vindicate the continuing place of the arts in the university curriculum. I therefore try to show that there is such a thing as the critical study of works of art and literature, and that this study discovers and transmits a legacy of moral knowledge. I explore some of the ways in which people, by judging works of art, become judges of themselves. This kind of judging has nothing to do with those fashionable "theories," from deconstruction to postmodernism, which have served to create such an impenetrable wall of jargon around our artistic heritage. It does not empty works of their life and meaning, or strive, like deconstruction, to show that meaning is impossible. It is a way of making works *live* in the imagination of their audience, so that art and audience belong together. And that relation of belonging is what we acquire through culture.

There is no point in studying culture, however, if you cannot also renew it. It is the failure to renew—indeed, the refusal to renew—that leads to the habit of repudiation, and to the attempt, through stultifying "theory," to set our literary and artistic heritage at an impassable distance from its intended audience. If we truly believed that this audience no longer exists, or that it could not be re-created, then we might reasonably give up on culture. Art, literature, music, and the humanities would be, for us, curious bundles deposited in the halls of scholarship. They would command no special discipline of study, and yield no special knowledge. We might turn upon them the frozen stare of "theory," but we would thereby discover only the dissected remnants of a corpse.

If culture is to be a valid subject of study, therefore, and a vehicle for judgment, it must be possible to identify the places, the people, and the practices in which it lives. I have tried to indicate a few developments, in which we can (without undue optimism) discern a new dawn after the night of repudiation, and a new attempt to recapture the ideals and emotions that have distinguished our civilization and justified its being in the world. I point to some of the ways in which the disasters of modernism and its postmodern aftermath are being overcome, as the old ways of simplicity and humility are recovered. This small scale work of renewal is far more important, it seems to me, than all the loud-mouthed blather of repudiation. It benefits those whose interests and education direct them towards art, literature, and philosophy. But it also benefits the entire civilization to which those people belong, and which depends in a thousand secret and not-so-secret ways on the transmission of cultural knowledge. To those who doubt this, I point to the example of Islam, contrasting what it was when it had a genuine culture with what it is today, when that culture is remembered only by powerless scholars, and belligerent ignorance is without the voices that might have corrected it.

1 | What Is Culture?

ANTHROPOLOGISTS WRITE OF the "culture" of the people they observe, meaning those customs and artifacts which are shared, and the sharing of which brings social cohesion. Ethnologists, on the one hand, define culture more widely, to include all intellectual, emotional, and behavioral features that are transmitted through learning and social interaction, rather than through genetic endowment. Sociologists, on the other hand, use the term more narrowly, to mean the thoughts and habits whereby people define their group identity, and stake out a claim for social territory. In all those uses, the term "culture" is associated with the human need for membership, and describes a shared asset of a social group. In this book I shall be defining "culture" in another way, to denote an acquisition that may not be shared by every member of a community, and which opens the hearts, minds, and senses of those who possess it to an intellectual and artistic patrimony. Culture, as I shall describe and defend it in this book, is the creation and creator of elites. This does not mean, however, that culture has nothing to do with membership or with the social need to define and conserve a shared way of life. Although an elite product, its meaning lies in emotions and aspirations that are common to all.

By "culture" I mean what has also been called "high

culture"—the accumulation of art, literature, and humane reflection that has stood the "test of time" and established a continuing tradition of reference and allusion among educated people. That definition raises a question: whose accumulation, and which people? In response, it is useful to revisit a distinction, made in another way and for another purpose by Herder, and exploited for yet another purpose by Spengler, between culture and civilization. A civilization is a social entity that manifests religious, political, legal, and customary uniformity over an extended period, and which confers on its members the benefits of socially accumulated knowledge. Thus, we can speak of Ancient Egyptian civilization, Roman civilization, Chinese civilization, and Western civilization. Civilizations can include each other, whether as contemporaneous or as successive parts. For example, Roman civilization includes that of Roman Gaul, and Islamic civilization that of the Abbasids.

The culture of a civilization is the art and literature through which it rises to consciousness of itself and defines its vision of the world. All civilizations have a culture, but not all cultures achieve equal heights. The stone-age civilization that produced the wall-paintings of the Lascaux caves has left a memorable icon of its world, but its one lasting cultural achievement pales beside the art and literature of Greece. Whether we can describe one culture as objectively superior to another is a question that I shall touch on later in this book. For the moment it is enough to recognize that cultures are the means through which civilizations become conscious of themselves, and are permeated by the strengths and weaknesses of their inherited form of life. There are as many cultures as there are civilizations, even though you can belong to a civilization and know little or nothing of its culture—which is the situation of most Westerners today.

WESTERN CULTURE

This book is about Western culture, which means the culture of Western civilization. To say as much is to set no clear limits to my topic. Civilizations grow out of and into each other, and often divide like amoebas so as to generate two contemporaneous offshoots; hence, it is very hard to set spatial or temporal boundaries on Western civilization. It grew from the fusion of Christianity with the law and government of Rome, became conscious of itself in the high Middle Ages, passed through a period of skepticism and Enlightenment, and was simultaneously spread around the globe by the trading and colonial interests of its more adventurous members. And throughout its most flourishing periods, Western civilization has produced a culture which happily absorbs and adapts the cultures of other places, other faiths, and other times. Its basic fund of stories, its moral precepts, and its religious imagery come from the Hebrew Bible and the Greek New Testament. Onto those Judeo-Christian roots, however, has been grafted a tree of many branches, bearing many kinds of fruit. *The Thousand and One Nights*, which has a central place in Islamic culture, is equally part of the cultural heritage of the West, while the pagan literature of Greece and Rome has been taught for centuries as the fount of our literary tradition.

Those facts should not make for confusion. There is no

paradox in the idea that two distinct cultures (belonging to two distinct civilizations) may nevertheless share parts of their heritage, and certainly no paradox in the idea that they can cross-fertilize each other, as Muslim, Christian, and Jewish cultures cross-fertilized each other in the great days of Averroës, Maimonides, and Peter Lombard. Indeed, it is important to understand, in the context of today's "culture wars" and the widespread advocacy of "multiculturalism," that Western culture has an unparalleled ability and willingness to assimilate other cultural traditions.

Still, it might be suggested that I have so far done very little to confine my subject matter. Are we really to consider all the art, literature, music, and philosophical reflection of the West as part of its culture, and does it all have a claim to our protection? Neither suggestion is plausible. Although new works are constantly being added to our inheritance, there is a distinction between those that "enter the canon" and those that remain on the periphery. Every culture is characterized by a central stream or tradition of works that have not merely "stood the test of time" but which continue to serve as models and inspirations for living practitioners. The process whereby an artistic, literary, or musical tradition develops and strengthens is a fascinating one, to which critics have devoted much thought. And theories of the "tradition" are invariably controversial, as critics fight to champion favorites of their own and to denigrate those of others. But this battle over the canon is itself part of the canon: a tradition is the residue of critical conflicts, that which remains when the sound and fury has dwindled to a schoolroom murmur.

CULTURE AND JUDGMENT

Another way of putting that point is to say that culture issues from judgment. A culture is supplied with its monuments and its durable styles by unceasing comparisons and choices, from which a canon of masterpieces emerges not as the object of a single collective choice, not even a choice that must be made anew by each generation, but as the by-product of myriad choices over centuries. Just as customs emerge over time, from the countless efforts of human beings to coordinate their conduct, so do cultural traditions emerge from the discussions, allusions, and comparisons, with which people fill their leisure hours.

Many people will be unhappy with that idea, believing either that there is no such thing as this "judgment" to which I refer or that, if there is such a thing, it is irremediably "subjective," with no inherent ability either to stand up to skeptical examination or to guarantee the survival of a culture in times of doubt. This response is expressed in a variety of ways and for a variety of purposes, and it is one aim of this book to rebut it. In all its forms, however, it rests on a confusion, long ago pointed out by Kant.[2] It is true that our judgments of works of art are subjective in the sense that they issue from our personal experience, impressions, and tastes. But it does not follow that they are subjective in the sense of admitting no argument in their favor, or connecting with no important experiences and emotions which might be tested by life.

Still, it might be wondered, what kind of judgment is intended? In considering this question, eighteenth-century writers referred to "taste," by which they meant a distinct

5

rational faculty, through which we choose what is worthy of our attention. But what kind of attention? And worthy in what respect? During the course of their discussions, thinkers of the Enlightenment began to write of "aesthetic" judgment, making use of a term introduced by Kant's mentor Baumgarten, though often disagreeing radically over what they meant by it. The term stuck, and today it is a commonplace to speak of aesthetic judgment as the thing that distinguishes the realm of culture from the realms of science, religion, and morality. We are, however, no nearer to a definition today than were those philosophers of the Enlightenment who, whether they stuck, like Hume and Addison, to the old idea of taste, or whether they adopted, like Kant and Schiller, the new jargon of aesthetics, were never able to satisfy one another that they were referring to a single thing.

JUDGMENT AND LAUGHTER

Rather than tie myself in that knot, therefore, I propose to cut through it by considering one of the raw materials from which culture is built, namely laughter. All rational beings laugh—and maybe only rational beings laugh. And all rational beings benefit from laughing. As a result there has emerged a peculiar human institution—that of the joke, the repeatable performance in words or gestures that is designed as an object of laughter. Now there is a great difficulty in saying exactly what laughter is. It is not just a sound—not even a sound, since it can be silent. Nor is it just a thought, like the thought of some object as incongruous. It is a response *to* something, which also involves a judgment *of* that thing. Moreover, it is not an individual peculiarity, like a nervous tic or a sneeze. Laughter is an expression of amusement, and amusement is an outwardly directed, socially pregnant state of mind.[3] Laughter begins as a collective condition, as when children giggle together over some absurdity. And in adulthood amusement remains one of the ways in which human beings enjoy each other's company, become reconciled to their differences, and accept their common lot. Laughter helps us to overcome our isolation and fortifies us against despair.

That does not mean that laughter is subjective in the sense that "anything goes," or that it is uncritical of its object. On the contrary, jokes are the object of fierce disputes, and many are dismissed as "not funny," "in bad taste," "offensive," and so on. The habit of laughing at things is not detachable from the habit of judging things to be worthy of laughter. Indeed, amusement, although a spontaneous outflow of social emotion, is also the most frequently practiced form of judgment. To laugh at something is already to judge it, and when we refrain from laughing at what someone nevertheless believes to be funny, we may thereby show our disapproval of that person's stance. A joke in "bad taste" is not just a failure: it is an offence, and one of the most important aspects of moral education is to teach children not to commit that offense. Think about this, and you will quickly see that, however difficult it may be to define such notions as "judgment" and "taste," they are absolutely indispensable to us.

Shakespeare provides us with a telling example of what I mean in the involved subplot to *Twelfth Night*. The drunken Sir Toby Belch and his disorderly companions decide to play a practical joke on Malvolio, steward to Sir Toby's beautiful cousin Olivia, in revenge for Malvolio's justified but stuck-up disapproval of their ways. The practical joke involves persuading Malvolio that Olivia loves him and will love him yet more if he obeys various absurd recommendations concerning his costume and conduct. As a result of this prank, Malvolio is at first humiliated, then wounded, and finally locked up as mad, to be rescued at last only by the twists and turns of the somewhat farcical plot. Remorse, of a shallow kind, visits the pranksters. But the audience, which had begun by laughing with them, finds itself now looking on them with cold disdain and on Malvolio with uneasy pity. A cloud of discomfiture surrounds the play's conclusion, as the laughter which had propelled it is suddenly brought to judgment and condemned.

THE CONCEPT OF ART

Those remarks do not amount to a theory of humor, or of the "judgment of taste" on which it depends. But they point to the fact that there is nothing obscure about this judgment, which is a familiar part of everybody's life, with a vital role to play in cementing human society. Maybe amusement is a species of, a cousin to, or a prelude to, aesthetic appreciation. But we don't have to determine whether that is so, in order to see that there really is a kind of judgment at the heart of culture, and that we are engaged in it all the time. Furthermore, this judgment can be educated, is in all forms morally relevant, and involves many of our deepest and most important social instincts. Reflecting on amusement and humor, and their place in our lives, you get a very clear intimation of a more general truth, about the nature and meaning of culture—namely that culture is judgment, and that judgment matters.

The example also helps us to deflect what has come to be a routine dismissal of culture and the pursuit of it—a dismissal that begins from skepticism about the concept of art. A century ago Marcel Duchamp signed a urinal, entitled it "La Fontaine," and then exhibited it as a work of art. This famous gesture has since been repeated *ad nauseam*, and insofar as students now learn anything in art schools, it consists in the ability to perform this gesture while believing it to be original—an epistemological achievement comparable to that of the White Queen who, in her youth, could believe six impossible propositions before breakfast. One immediate result of Duchamp's joke was to precipitate an intellectual industry devoted to answering the question "What is art?" The literature of this industry is as tedious and pointless as are the imitations of Duchamp's gesture, and not even the wit and intellect of Arthur Danto has served to enliven it.[4] Nevertheless, it has left a residue of skepticism that has fueled the attack on culture. If anything can count as art, then art ceases to have a point. All that is left is the curious but unfounded fact that some people like looking at some things, others like looking at others. As for the suggestion that there is an enterprise of criticism, which searches for objective values and lasting monuments to the human spirit, this is dismissed out of hand as depending on a conception of the artwork that was washed down the drain of Duchamp's "fountain."

The argument has been rehearsed with malicious wit by

John Carey,[5] and is fast becoming orthodoxy, not least because it seems to emancipate people from the burden of culture, telling them that all those venerable masterpieces can be ignored with impunity, that reality T V is "as good as" Shakespeare and techno-rock the equal of Brahms, since nothing is better than anything else and all claims to aesthetic value are void. The argument, however, is based on the elementary mistake of thinking of art as what Mill called a "natural kind," like water, calcium carbonate, or the tiger—in other words, a kind whose essence is fixed not by human interests, but by the way things are.[6] If, in defining art, we were attempting to isolate some feature of the natural order, then our definition would certainly have failed if we could set no limits to the concept. "Art," however, is not the name of a natural kind, but of a functional kind, like "table." Anything is a table if it can be used as tables are used —to support things at which we sit to work or eat. A packing case can be a table; an old urinal can be a table; a human slave can be a table. This does not make the concept arbitrary, nor does it prevent us from distinguishing good tables from bad.

Return now to the example of jokes. It is as hard to circumscribe the class of jokes as it is the class of artworks. Anything is a joke if somebody says so. For "joke" names a functional kind. A joke is an artifact made to be laughed at. It may fail to perform its function, in which case it is a joke that "falls flat." Or it may perform its function, but offensively, in which case it is a joke "in bad taste." But none of this implies that the category of jokes is arbitrary, or that there is no such thing as a distinction between good jokes and bad. Nor does it in any way suggest that there is no place for the criticism of jokes, or for the kind of moral education that has a dignified and decorous sense of humor as its goal. Indeed, the first thing you might learn, in considering jokes, is that Marcel Duchamp's urinal was one—quite a good one the first time around, corny by mid-twentieth century, and downright stupid today.

ART AND AESTHETIC INTEREST

What I have said about jokes can be readily transferred to artworks too. Anything is art if somebody sincerely says so, for art is a functional kind. A work of art is something put forward as an object of aesthetic interest. It may fail to perform its function, in which case it is aesthetically empty. Or it may perform its function, but offensively, in which case it is brash, vulgar, disturbing, or whatever. But none of this implies that the category of art is arbitrary, or that there is no such thing as a distinction between good and bad art. Still less does it suggest that there is no place for the criticism of art, or for the kind of aesthetic education that has a decorous and humane aesthetic understanding as its goal.

It is hardly surprising that jokes and artworks are so similar. For some artworks consist entirely of jokes: not only cheeky gestures like Duchamp's urinal, but also extended works of literature, like *Tristram Shandy* and *Through the Looking Glass*. Comedies and jokes appeal to the same emotional repertoire. And jokes, like works of art, can be endlessly repeatable. Still, in defining art as a functional kind I have introduced a new idea—that of "aesthetic interest." And the reader will want to know what kind of interest this is, and whether it is central to culture in general, or specialized to works of art. This is another knot which I propose to cut through. Aesthetic interest, I suggest, is simply the kind of interest that we take in works of art. We are all familiar with it, though we don't necessarily know how to define it. And we all know that, like amusement, aesthetic interest is inseparable from judgment.

Works of art, like jokes, are objects of perception: it is how they look, how they sound, how they appeal to our sensory perception, that matters. In aesthetic interest we see the world as it really seems: in Wallace Stevens's words we "let be be finale of seem." We then encounter a unity of experience and thought, a coming together of the sensory and the intellectual for which "imagination" is the everyday name. This fact, which places the meaning of aesthetic experience outside the reach of science, explains its peculiar value. In the moment of beauty we encounter meaning in immediate and sensory form.

Aesthetic interest is of the greatest practical import to beings like us, who move on the surface of things. To engage now with those distant parts of my life which are not of immediate concern, to absorb into the present choice the full reality of a life that stretches into distant moral space, I need insight into the meaning of things. I need symbols in the present moment, of matters beyond the moment. The ability to participate imaginatively in merely possible states of affairs is one of the gifts of culture: without this ability a person may not know what it is like to achieve the goals at which he aims, and his pursuit of those goals will be to a certain measure irrational.[7]

Aesthetic interest is an interest in appearances. But there are appearances that we ought to avoid, however much they fascinate us. By contrast, there are appearances which are not merely permissible objects of aesthetic interest, but which reward that interest with knowledge, understanding, and emotional uplift. We deplore the Roman games, at which animals are slaughtered, prisoners crucified, and innocents tormented, all for the sake of the spectacle and its gruesome meaning. And we would deplore it, even if the suffering were simulated, as in some cinematic replication, if we thought that the interest of the observer were merely one of gleeful fascination. But we praise the Greek tragedy, in which profound myths are enacted in lofty verse, in which the imagined deaths take place out of sight and unrelished by the audience. An interest in the one, we suppose, is depraved, in the other noble. And a high culture aims, or ought to aim, at preserving and enhancing experiences of the second kind, in which human life is raised to a higher level—the level of ethical reflection.

THE SPHERE OF CULTURE

A culture does not comprise works of art only, nor is it directed solely to aesthetic interests. It is the sphere of *intrinsically interesting artifacts*, linked by the faculty of judgment to our aspirations and ideals. We appreciate jokes, works of art, arguments, works of history and literature, manners, dress, and forms of behavior. And all these things are shaped through judgment.

What should we include in the category of culture? The answer is suggested by my argument, which has pointed to a certain kind of judgment as central to the phenomenon. A culture consists of all those activities and artifacts which are organized by the "common pursuit of true judgment," as T. S. Eliot once put it.[8] And true judgment involves the search for meaning through the reflective encounter with things made, composed, and written, with such an end in view. Some of those things will be works of art, addressed to the aesthetic interest; others will be discursive works of history or philosophy, addressed to the interest in ideas. Both kinds of work explore the meaning of the world and the life of society. And the purpose of both is to stimulate the judgments through which we understand each other and ourselves.

Artistic and philosophical traditions therefore provide our paradigm of culture. And the principle that organizes a tradition also discriminates within it, creating the canon of masterpieces, the received monuments, the "touchstones" as Matthew Arnold once called them, which it is the goal of humane education to appreciate and to understand.[9] The question now before us is how we might justify such an education, and what should be its place in the curriculum today.

Before addressing that question, however, there is an objection that must be acknowledged. Many people with no interest in high culture make moral judgments. They judge people in terms of their characters and actions, and organize their world through conceptions of right and wrong, good and bad, virtue and vice. Yet the species of judgment that I have been considering, which looks critically on the forms of human interest, and which searches the world for meanings, implications, and allusions, may hold no interest for them. Their taste in art, like their taste in jokes, may be coarse or nonexistent; their interest in ideas and arguments may be equally sparse, and the only spectacles they enjoy might be those of organized sport. Yet this says nothing about their moral worth, or their utility as members of society. Conversely, there are highly cultivated people, with a refined taste in art and consuming interest in intellectual questions, who live the lives of vicious psychopaths: Hitler and Stalin, to name but two. These evident facts, repeatedly and lamentably confirmed by history, lend a new kind of force to the cultural skeptic, who may still ask what the point is of activities and interests that leave the moral landscape seemingly so little changed. This is, I suspect, the principal reservation that educated people may have, concerning the value of culture and the purpose of teaching it. It will therefore be necessary for me to return, in the course of my argument, to the problem posed by the "evil aesthete," and the "philistine philanthropist"—the problem of the seeming disconnection between moral virtue and cultural refinement.

2 | Leisure, Cult, and Culture

CULTURE IS THE product of leisure: it is created and enjoyed in those moments, or those states of mind, when the immediate urgencies of practical life are in abeyance. Our culture was, historically, the product of a leisured class —a class with a virtual monopoly on leisure. But today we live in a society in which leisure is universally available, even to those who lack a use for it. This is one cause of the deep uncertainty about "Western culture." There seems a radical disjunction between our aristocratic and high-bourgeois inheritance, the product of an educated class of priests, prophets, and noblemen, and the works of our newly emancipated "common man"—whose fanfare, however, was composed by Aaron Copland, a most uncommon member of the educated elite. In order to clarify our predicament, it is worth reflecting on leisure, and its connection with religion on the one hand, and culture on the other.

LEISURE, PLAY, AND THE AESTHETIC

The Greeks took leisure seriously, a fact recorded in the subsequent history of their word for it—*schole*—which became *scola* in Latin, and school in English. Leisure, for Aristotle, was the purpose of work—not work in the sense of any specific activity but in the general sense of *ascholia* (leisurelessness).[10]

Ascholia was Aristotle's term for business, and it has its equivalent in Latin (*neg-otium*), and survives, too, in French. The *negociant* is the one who is always busy, and who therefore has the question before him: why? What purpose is served by business, and when is that purpose fulfilled? For Aristotle the answer was clear: you work in order to free yourself for leisure, and in leisure you are truly free: free to pursue the contemplative life which, for Aristotle, was the highest good.

In that account you see a radically different set of priorities from those that animate a modern economy. Work, for Aristotle, is mere "leisurelessness," a condition of lack, which we strive to overcome so as to enjoy our true human fulfilment, which is the life of contemplation. This emphasis on contemplation may seem like so much philosophical snobbery. What Aristotle had in mind, however, was an activity which is its own reward, and which therefore illustrates the condition of contentment. For the philosopher, the question "Why contemplate?" neither has nor deserves an answer. Contemplation is not a means to an end, but an end in itself. And this, Aristotle implies, is what all true *schole* involves.

For a great many people today leisure is not a state of contemplation but one of physical activity—although activity which, like Aristotle's contemplation, is *its own reward*. Recreation, sport, and games are all to be understood in the spirit of Aristotle's *schole*—as activities which are not means to an end but ends in themselves. That is why these activities, however strenuous, are activities in which we are *at rest*: for our plans and projects *come to rest* in them. This, we are apt to say, is the point of it all, what we worked for, the goal to which our labor was a means.

What I am saying about leisure was said, in another tone of voice but for a connected purpose, by Schiller, not about leisure but about play, which is its prototype in the world of the child. In his *Letters on the Aesthetic Education of Man*,[11] Schiller described play as the higher condition to which we aspire whenever we relinquish our practical concerns. The contrast he had in mind was not that between play and work, but that between playing and being in earnest. And he used that distinction to make an interesting remark about aesthetics. "With the good and the useful," he wrote, "man is merely in earnest; but with the beautiful he plays." That phrase "merely in earnest" is of course heavily ironic, but it expresses a systematic rejection of the workaday world. Fulfillment does not come through purpose, Schiller is implying, but only when purpose is set aside. And for Schiller, the paradigm of fulfilment is the aesthetic experience—not contemplation as Aristotle understood it, but the disinterested contemplation of *appearances*, the self-conscious alertness to *the presented meaning* of things.

Schiller believed that we can understand aesthetic judgment if we refer it back to the world of play—a world in which nothing really has a purpose, and where every action is engaged in for its own sake, as something intrinsically delightful. Art returns us to that world of primal innocence, by enabling us to set our purposes aside. It is not merely that the work of art is valued for its own sake, and without reference to a purpose. It is also that we, in the act of appreciation, reassume the mantle of a child, allowing our emotions and impressions to follow imaginative paths, constraining them to no purpose, no goal, no earnest endeavor. And just as a child learns through play, so do we learn through the aesthetic experience, by exercising our feelings in imaginary realms, enlarging our vision of humanity, and coming to see the world as imbued with intrinsic values, meaningful in itself and without reference to our own self-centered interests.

LEISURE AND DISTRACTION

Schiller saw culture as the sphere of "aesthetic education," and play as its archetype. And through uniting the two ideas he hoped to show that the decline of religion had not bereft mankind of intrinsic values. Through "aesthetic education" —in other words, culture—we could reconnect to those primordial experiences of wonder and awe which show us the lasting meaning of our life on earth. That is why culture matters: it is a vessel in which intrinsic values are captured and handed on.

Aristotle and Schiller both emphasize the active nature of leisure and its connection to contemplative forms of mental life. But we can switch off from work without switching on to any higher purpose. We can pass from activity to passivity, in which our mind does not engage the world but is rather engaged by it, distracted by external things rather than interested in them. And someone might suggest that distraction is more and more the normal position of people when their work is set aside. Television techniques are increasingly designed to capture attention, rather than to provide a point of interest, and recent research[12] has demonstrated the extent to which the normal channels of information gathering have been short-circuited by TV, producing widespread attention disorders and an addiction to visual stimulation. If this is leisure, many people say, let's have less of it.

The distinction between distraction and interest is hard to draw exactly. After all, you cannot be distracted by something without also being interested in it. But the interest stops with the next distraction. The mind does not *keep hold* of the first object of attention, since it is incapable of pursuing its interest if the stimulus is not renewed. Art lovers standing before a painting look and look, and even when they look away, their thoughts are of the picture. Each detail interests them; each shape and colour has a meaning, and they search the picture for a human significance that they may try to put into words, if they are critically inclined, or which they may store silently in their hearts. Here all the attention comes from the viewers: they are actively engaged in interpreting what they see, and their viewing is in a certain measure a creative act. They are creating the object of their own awareness, but also receiving from it a vision of repose.

By contrast the couch potato in front of the television screen, his eyes led from image to image by the five-second cut, is barely able to attend to one thing before his mind is captured by another. Here there is still scope for mental activity—for example, a judgment of the aesthetic, moral, or philosophical worth of the scene on the screen. But the object of attention is not the product of this mental activity, and stays in view only because it is able constantly to distract the mind of the viewer from its previous focus.

The TV is a paradigm of the distracting process, but it is not the only instance. Many forms of popular entertainment have a similar character, of diverting attention while neutralizing thought. And when sociologists speak of the "recreational" use of drugs, alcohol, and other things (sex included), they are really talking of distraction. Recreation, in this sense, means maintaining mental vacancy, even in the midst of activities like sex, which require the full engagement of the person if they are to deliver what they mean. If popular entertainment is mere distraction, then we might reasonably suggest that leisure, in the sense intended by Aristotle, has vanished from the world of popular entertainment, that the final emancipation of the workers from their work has led to the loss of the one thing that they were really working for.

Sport and Spectacle

There are, however, popular entertainments which strive to neutralize distraction and to put involvement in its place. Spectator sport is one important instance. The pleasure of the football fan comes from a vicarious involvement with the players, acting out in imagination what the team is going through in fact. This is active contemplation, fully engaging the faculties. In the case of American football, we witness a ritualization of the event that raises it from the ludic to the quasi-religious level. Here the spectators are as much part of the event as the congregation is part of a religious ceremony. The marching bands in their uniforms, the scintillating flags of the crowd, the cheerleaders bouncing and bobbing with an unselfconscious delight in being alive that is purely American, and the atmosphere of easygoing pride in an event that is also nothing in particular—all this raises spectator sport to the level of ritual, with a combination of the sacred and the everyday that is not unlike that exhibited by religious ceremonies. You will be reminded of the Olympian Odes of Pindar, in which the virtues of athletes are extolled through the myths of the gods. And you will understand the etymology of "holiday" and the need in every society for days that are set aside as such, when—because work is forbidden—all activity is seen in another light.

CULTURE AND CULT

What I have just described is another use of leisure: one in which leisure means not activity but the involvement in a spectacle, valued for its meaning as an end in itself. This involvement was once imbued with far-reaching mythical and religious meanings, and even today awakens some of the passions associated with the cults of gods and heroes. And it points to another connection—not that between leisure and culture, but that between leisure and cult.

In the Book of Genesis is told the story of God's creation of the world, expressed with admirable succinctness and simplicity, and through imagery which recreates some of that primordial wonder which we witness also in the Lascaux caves. And on the seventh day, the story tells us, God rested, thereby setting an example to his creatures who, in honor of all those things that are ends in themselves, of which their Creator is the supreme example, devote one day a week to worshipping Him. This, their day of recreation, is also a day of re-creation, in which the spirit is renewed, and the meaning of life unfolded.

This story points to an important feature of human

communities, though one that is not easily observed in the modern world. In the spirit of Genesis, we might indulge in our own fanciful genealogy of the human condition, and one more in keeping, perhaps, with modern science. Imagine, then, a hunter-gatherer community, which tracks its large quarry for several days and finally triumphs. The community can rest at last, can gather round together for a feast, but it will experience also a flow of gratitude, perhaps offering the first burnt morsel to a god. All kinds of explanations have been offered for the ancient practice of ritual sacrifice.[13] But perhaps the simplest and most plausible is that it is the survival of that primitive feast, in which the gods were summoned down among their worshippers, so as to taste the gifts that they themselves provided. Later—agricultural —communities did not need to hunt for their meals, but the need for ceremonial killing, for gratitude and feasting, was by then immovable. And something of this survives in the feast of 'Eid, in the Christian Communion, in the Jewish Passover, and in the Chinese festival of the New Year.

In time, we might suppose, the gods detached themselves from the feasts in which they were revealed, to become objects of theological study. But their festivals remained, as the principal way in which communities rehearsed their membership, through recreational activities that restored the shared meaning of their world. One such festival was that devoted to Dionysus in Athens, when poets competed for the approval of the crowd with their tragic tales of gods and heroes. And some of these tragedies survive, examples of the highest art and testimony to a long tradition of speculation and insight.

Culture Counts

That genealogy is, of course, a fiction. But it is, I believe, an illuminating fiction, one that spells out in time the timeless connections between contiguous things. It takes us from the species-needs of the hunter-gatherer to the birth of revealed religion, thence to organized worship and the communal festival and finally to culture as a genial byproduct of our festive celebrations. The connection between cult and culture can be made in other ways,[14] but its intrinsic plausibility is displayed in the story that I told, and that story prompts the following thought:

Culture grows from religion, and religion from a species-need. But the culture engendered by a religion may also turn upon its parent with a skeptical eye. This has often happened, and indeed was already happening in the Greek theater. Not only were the gods and heroes lampooned by Aristophanes; their solemn stories were told by Aeschylus and Euripides with an air of detachment, as allegories of the human condition rather than literal descriptions of immortal goings-on.

Not that the tragedians disbelieved in the gods. Judging from their surviving works, they neither believed nor disbelieved, regarding belief as in some way irrelevant to their task, which was to capture and illustrate the *meaning of the world*. Like Plato and Socrates, they saw the stories of the gods as myths, and treated myth as another mode of knowledge, distinct from both rational science and storytelling. They believed in God rather than the gods, and their God was, like that of Plato, Socrates, and Aristotle, infinite, eternal, inscrutable, standing in judgment over a world that does not really contain Him.

———

GROWING AWAY FROM RELIGION

The tendency of high culture to detach itself from its religious origin can be witnessed in many places and at many times. The Augustan poets of Rome are already standing back from their religious inheritance, with Lucretius expressly pouring scorn on it. The Sufi poets of Persia (Hafiz, Rumi, and Omar Khayyam), profoundly religious though their sentiments are, have only an awkward and tangential relation to the Islamic orthodoxies of their surrounding society. Shakespeare's plays neither endorse nor condemn the Christian vision, but stand at such a distance from it as to prompt the views that he was an atheist, a pagan, a Protestant, and even a Catholic recusant, each interpretation compellingly illustrated from the texts.[15] And since the Enlightenment it has been clear that poetry, music, and art—while they may often express profound religious faith—are equally able to continue in a spirit of skepticism, invoking the values of community and endowing all that they touch with a spiritual nimbus, while at the same time refraining from any commitment to theological doctrine or even pouring scorn on that doctrine, in the manner of Diderot, Shelley, and Nietzsche.

This process of "growing away" from religion creates the great divide between the leisure interests of ordinary people and the culture of the critical elite. In the conditions of scarcity from which civilizations begin, the religious festival and the weekly worship are the only times in which the spirit of leisure can possess the ordinary person—and they are times dedicated to religion, and to the affirmation of the community through ritual, song, and prayer. But, as the mastery over the environment advances, so does leisure increase. And while the elite devotes this newly abundant leisure to contemplation and high culture, ordinary people use it to engage in forms of recreation and distraction remote from the contemplative ideal espoused by Aristotle. The extreme point has been reached today, in which neither the elite culture nor popular entertainment belong to the practice of religion, but where both, in secret or not-so-secret ways, bear the impress of religion, and carry into the world of enlightened common sense that now surrounds us, precious canisters of the intriguing darkness from which humanity began and for which some part of us still yearns.

Even at its most atheistic, however, Western art has shown a great respect for myth, seeing it as the Greek tragedians saw it—a vehicle by which the deep truths of the human condition can be conveyed in allegorical form. Wagner rewrote the Germanic myths and medieval legends, incorporating them into works of art expressly modeled on the tragedies of Aeschylus. Since then the idea has been common among artists that their task is to represent the spiritual truth of the human condition by deploying old myths in novel ways. Art has gradually taken over from religion the task of symbolizing the spiritual realities that elude the reach of science. In this way, as religion has lost its hold over the collective imagination, culture has come to seem increasingly important, being the most reliable channel through which exalted ethical ideas can enter the minds of skeptical people.

My argument in this chapter therefore leaves us with a host of awkward questions: can culture really serve as a religion substitute? Is it right that it should do so? Are there not better uses for our leisure time? Are there good and bad ways of teaching culture, and is there a cultural curriculum best suited to the kind of knowledge that culture conveys? All of these questions demand us to explore the nature of human knowledge, and the ways in which it can be conserved, enhanced, and passed on.

3 | Knowledge and Feeling

IT IS ONE of the most deeply rooted superstitions of our age that the purpose of education is to benefit those who receive it. What we teach in school, what subjects we encourage in universities, and the methods of instruction, are all subject to the one overarching test: what do the kids get out of it? And this test soon gives way to another, yet more pernicious in its effect, but no less persuasive in the thinking of educationists: is it relevant? And by "relevant" is invariably meant "relevant to the interests of the kids themselves." From these superstitions have arisen all the recipes for failure that have dominated our educational systems: the proliferation of ephemeral subjects, the avoidance of difficulties, methods of teaching that strive to maintain interest at all costs—even at the cost of knowledge. Whether we put the blame on Rousseau, whose preposterous book *Émile* began the habit of sentimentalizing the process whereby knowledge is transferred from one brain to another, on John Dewey, whose hostility to "rote learning" and old-fashioned discipline led to the fashion for "child-centered learning," or simply on the egalitarian ideas which were bound to sweep through our schools when teachers were no longer properly remunerated—in whatever way we apportion blame, it is clear that we have entered a period of rapid educational decline, in which some people learn masses, but the masses learn little or nothing at all.

THE GOAL OF KNOWLEDGE

The superstition that I referred to is, in a certain measure, the opposite of the truth. True teachers do not provide knowledge as a benefit to their pupils; they treat their pupils as a benefit to knowledge. Of course they love their pupils, but they love knowledge more. And their overriding concern is to pass on that knowledge by lodging it in brains that will last longer than their own. Their methods are not "child-centered" but "knowledge-centered," and the focus of their interest is the subject, rather than the things that might make that subject for the time being "relevant" to matters of no intellectual concern. Any attempt to make education relevant risks reducing it to those parts that are of relevance to the uneducated—which are invariably the parts with the shortest lifespan. A relevant curriculum is one from which the difficult core of knowledge has been excised, and while it may be relevant now it will be futile in a few years' time. Conversely irrelevant-seeming knowledge, when properly acquired, is not merely a discipline that can be adapted and applied; it is likely to be exactly what is needed, in circumstances that nobody foresaw. The "irrelevant" sciences of Boolean algebra and Fregean logic gave birth, in time, to the digital computer; the "irrelevant" studies of Greek, Latin, and ancient history enabled a tiny number of British graduates to govern an Empire that stretched around the world, while the "irrelevant" paradoxes of Kant's *Critique of Pure*

Reason caused the theory of relativity to dawn in the mind of Albert Einstein.

It is worth saying all that, not only because the superstitions to which I refer are so deeply rooted in our modern ways of thinking, but also because those who adopt them will never see the educational value of culture, and will never have a clue as to how it might be taught. What does it benefit ordinary children that they should know the works of Shakespeare, acquire a taste for Bach, or develop an interest in medieval Latin? All such attainments merely isolate a child from his peers, place a veil between his thinking and the only world where he can apply it, and are at best an eccentricity, at worst a handicap. My reply is simple: it may not benefit the child—not yet, at least. But it will benefit culture. And because culture is a form of knowledge, it is the business of the teacher to look for the pupil who will pass it on.

Types of Knowledge

To make good that reply, however, I must say a little about knowledge. When we say that Mary knows something, we imply that her way of thinking and acting is responsive to the way things are, so that her judgment is reliable and her actions blessed with success. Thus if I say, "She really knows this stuff," patting a book of physics, you can take it that Mary is someone who could tell you the facts about physics. Likewise, when I point to her in the dressage arena and say, "She really knows what she is doing," you will infer that, if you follow her example, you too will ride a horse. The topic of knowledge is hotly disputed among philosophers, but that much at least is agreed. And it explains why knowledge is important, and why human beings have developed procedures and institutions for acquiring it and passing it on. Knowledge gained is a gain for all of us; knowledge lost, a loss that all must bear. It does not matter who possesses the knowledge: the important thing is that it should be there, publicly available, and that human beings should know how to recuperate it from the common fund. That is what education does for us: it keeps knowledge alive, by endowing people with the ability to summon it, either because they have internalized it like Mary, or because they have learned to unlock the books and records in which it is sequestered. That textbook of physics may contain all the knowledge that we need about its subject matter, but without Mary and people like her this knowledge will be lost—and maybe lost forever. You and I have a key to that knowledge, which is: "Ask Mary." But unless someone really "knows this stuff," books and records are no better than the book of nature, which stares at us mutely until we rediscover the spell that makes it speak.

It is sometimes said that we now live in a "knowledge economy," and that "information technology" has vastly increased the extent and accessibility of human knowledge. Both claims are false. "Information technology" simply means the use of digital algorithms in the transference of messages. The "information" that is processed is not information *about* anything, nor does it have its equivalent in knowledge. It treats truth and falsehood, reality and fantasy, as equivalent, and has no means to assess the difference. Indeed, as the Internet reveals, information technology is far more effective in propagating ignorance than in advancing science. For, in the conquest of cyberspace, ignorance

31

has a flying start, being adapted to the habits of idle minds. Similarly, the claim that we exist in a "knowledge economy" is entirely unfounded. The effect of information technology is to give images precedence over thought and to multiply a thousand-fold the noise that fills the space in which ideas are conceived and brokered. Hence, when it comes to the great decisions, noise drowns out the still small voice of understanding. It was knowledge that enabled those 1,000 British civil servants to govern the vast subcontinent of India, or a comparable number of Roman citizens to bring law and order to the entire civilized world. It was knowledge painfully acquired from books and acquired in silence —and it was acquired because the competing noise had been carefully filtered out by educational institutions that created a common frame of reference among those who attended them. America today has several million civil servants, engaged in multiplying and perpetuating each others' mistakes, and the cause of this is information.

There is another reason for distrusting the easy equation of information with knowledge, which is that it represents knowledge as a single kind of thing. The paradigm proposed is that of factual knowledge, the kind of knowledge that can be contained in a textbook and deployed by the person who understands what the textbook says. But that is only one kind of knowledge, and a comparative latecomer to the scene of human instruction. There is also practical knowledge—the knowledge that shows itself in the skills of the hunter-gatherer or the soldier, and equally in the ability to nurse, to support, and to console. Greek philosophers distinguished, in this connection, *theoria* from *praxis*, arguing that both are exercises of the rational mind. For just as there are reasons for believing, so are there reasons for action, and while the first count towards the truth of what is believed, the second count towards the rightness of what is done. The person with knowledge is the one who can be relied upon to guide us towards reason's goal, which is truth in the one case, rightness in the other.

In ordinary language we make a distinction between knowing that and knowing *how*, and the philosopher Gilbert Ryle pinpointed this fact as a kind of warrant for the ancient distinction.[16] I know that the earth goes round the sun, and I know how to ride a bicycle. The first is knowledge of a fact, the second knowledge of a technique. And clearly I can know how to ride a bicycle even if I haven't the faintest idea of the theory which explains why bicycles stay upright when ridden. Conversely I can be entirely conversant with the theory, and have no ability to stay aloft on a bicycle.

ENDS AND MEANS

If that were all that the distinction between theoretical and practical knowledge amounted to, we should be hard-pressed to find a place for culture in the curriculum. We should have on the one hand the hard sciences—like physics, chemistry, and math—together with history and geography, all of which deal in facts. And, on the other hand, we should have technical disciplines—engineering, craft, and sports. Languages, which involve both factual knowledge and practical skills, would form a kind of intermediate zone, but culture would be nowhere on the curriculum. What facts do you learn from Chaucer other than the fact that he wrote those poems? And what skills has a medieval Englishman to communicate, through his poetry, to the busy children of today?

Surely, however, there is more to practical knowledge than skills and techniques. Someone who has mastered the military arts may use them for good ends or bad, and the same is true of any skill. Yet there is something more to be learned, when we learn a skill, which is how to make proper use of it. The good soldier, as this character was drawn in literature, was not merely someone who had mastered the arts of warfare; he was someone for whom the sense of honor and duty governed all that he did, in whom impatience with insults and challenges was tempered by chivalry and the desire to protect. In short, he was someone with a specific set of military virtues—virtues that might very well lead him into danger or into other kinds of trouble[17], but which attracted to him the admiration and affection of those who depended upon his courage and his skills.

Some philosophers speak, in this connection, of a distinction between knowledge of means, and knowledge of ends; for Aristotle the distinction was that between skill and virtue. Whichever language we choose, we find ourselves embroiled in the deepest philosophical controversy. Can there really be such a thing as practical knowledge, when what is at stake is not technique or skill, but the purposes to which we apply them? Is there really such a thing as aiming in ignorance, and such a thing as aiming knowledgeably? And is *that* the difference between the bad person and the good, namely a difference in *knowledge*?

Cutting through this knot is not easy. But ordinary language offers us another clue. We recognize not only knowledge *that* and knowledge *how*, but also knowledge *what*, and this idiom seems to be irreducible to either of the others. You are sitting in your office and a colleague storms in and baselessly accuses you of insulting her. Reporting the episode afterwards you say "I didn't know what to do." What kind of ignorance are you referring to? You come home from your husband's funeral, sweep with desolate eyes the house that you had shared with him, sit empty and forlorn on the couch, and then suddenly you "know what to do": there are friends to write to, tasks to complete, and the string quartet you were rehearsing for a concert.

This "knowing what to do" looks very like what philosophers have had in mind in referring to knowledge of ends. It is not just a matter of knowing how to go about some existing purpose; it is a matter of having the right purpose, the purpose appropriate to the situation in hand. Of course, there is a difficulty presented by that word "appropriate." But we are not without intuitions as to what it means. The inappropriate action is marked by a certain kind of failure: it peters out, stumbles into confusion, makes the situation worse than it might have been. Conversely, the appropriate action is the one that rescues what can be rescued, which brings success where success is feasible, leads on from one affirmative to another, so that the agent is never nonplussed or thwarted in his aims. In short, this kind of "knowing what" has to do with success in action. The one who "knows what to do" is the one on whom you can rely to make the best shot at success, whenever success is possible.

———

Knowing What to Feel

But there is another application of the phrase "knowing *what*," which is even more pertinent to my theme: knowing what to feel. When your colleague burst in to your office that day to plaster you with gratuitous insults, you didn't know what to feel—anger, puzzlement, fear, pity, all "crossed your mind," but none took possession of it. When, coming home from the walk which had begun when you stormed out in anger from a marital quarrel, you find your husband dead on the living room floor—then, too, perhaps, you don't know what to feel. And maybe for days afterwards you remain numb, cold, barely sentient with the shock of it. Even people whose responses are entirely normal can find themselves, in such a situation, not "knowing what to feel," and looking for a way forward that will help them.

There are forms of "knowing how" which involve "knowing what." Knowing how to console another is not simply a matter of skill. It involves knowing what to feel, as well as knowing how to express that feeling in words and gestures. It means being able to sympathize, while retaining sufficient distance to judge just how much sympathy would be right, and towards what aspect of the other's predicament. In general it is in the workings of sympathy that our emotions undergo their severest test: the temptation is to retreat from the spectacle of suffering, or else to sentimentalize and so to deny the reality. Learning what to feel in the face of another's grief or distress is one of the hardest aspects of moral education.

I shall take for granted this idea of knowing what to feel,

and hope that subsequent arguments will persuade you that there really is such a thing, and that it is critical to moral education. The two kinds of "knowing what" are not as distinct as I have implied. Knowing what to do means being rightly motivated, and right motivation means right feeling. The connections here are deep, and it was Aristotle who first tried to spell them out, arguing that right action springs from virtue, and that virtue is a habit in which a distinctive motive is embedded. That motive requires, in turn, a kind of order in one's emotions, an ability to feel rightly, towards the right object in the right degree. Thus the good-tempered person is one who is "angry at the right things and with the right people, and further, as he ought, when he ought, and as long as he ought."[18] In general, to teach virtue we must educate the emotions, and this means learning "what to feel" in the various circumstances that prompt them. The virtuous person, in Aristotle's understanding, does not merely know what to do and what to feel: his life and actions are imbued with the kind of success which is the reward of rational beings, and which Aristotle described as *eudaimonia*, a term normally translated as happiness or fulfillment.

Teaching Virtue

How is virtue taught? Aristotle's answer is simple: by imitation. But the answer is too simple. For we can imitate virtuous actions only if we are in a position that calls for them. Rudimentary justice, rudimentary courage, and the day-to-day forms of prudence and temperance are, of course, constantly called for. But the testing experiences, the difficult temptations, the human complexities which may one day beset us are things that we encounter only when it is too late to acquire the virtues that will see us through. Maybe, by practicing virtue in our small corner of the world, we will be more ready to practice it in the great field of human conflict. Even if that is not so, we can nevertheless gain the knowledge of *what to feel*, in those testing circumstances. We cannot be sure, when the time comes, that we shall feel as we ought, but we can rehearse in imagination the knowledge that we might one day require.

For instance, we can read stories of the heroes and their adventures; we can study narratives of historical exploits, and look at pictures of the life that we share. We can listen to homilies and rehearse in ritual form the joys and sufferings of revered and exemplary people. In all kinds of ways the emotions and motives of other people "come before us" in works of art and culture, and we spontaneously sympathize, by recreating in imagination the life that they depict. It is not that we imitate the characters depicted, but that we "move with" them, acquiring an inner premonition of their motives, and coming to see those motives in the context that the writer or artist provides. Through imagination we reach emotional knowledge, and maybe this is the best way, in the advance of the crucial tests, of preparing ourselves for the joys and calamities that we will some day encounter.

Much of this imaginative education is conducted through religion. Rationalists tend to think of religious education as involving the transmission of doctrines about God, man, and creation—doctrines, they believe, that do not stand up to scientific examination, and which in any case hardly fit those who accept them for membership of a skeptical modern community. In fact religious education down the ages has been very little concerned with doctrine. Its main message has been contained in rituals, maxims, and stories, and the goal of all three is moral education—teaching what to do, and more importantly, what to feel, in the circumstances of ordinary human life. The goal of religious education is, on the one hand, the cultivation of the heart, not the head, and the doctrines make sense of that other knowledge, a knowledge that we acquire more easily through ritual, and through holy words and examples, than through any form of theory. On the other hand—and here lies the deep difference between religion and culture—the education of the emotions through religion occurs only when the doctrines are believed. That is why culture cannot be a religion substitute, even though, in a sense, religion is a culture substitute in the lives of those who lack "aesthetic education."

CONSERVING PRACTICAL KNOWLEDGE

Let us return now to the thoughts from which this chapter began. I emphasized that we make a mistake in believing that education exists primarily to benefit its recipient. I suggested, rather, that the goal of education is to preserve our communal store of knowledge, and to keep open the channels through which we can call on it when we need to. This may seem a more plausible suggestion when referring to knowledge *that* than when referring to knowledge *how* or *what*. Practical knowledge seems far more intimately bound up with the circumstances of its use than theoretical knowledge. Nevertheless, it is true of practical knowledge, too, that we educate people in order to conserve it, and if we ever lose sight of this truth, then we are sure to lose what practical knowledge we have. If ever we think that we teach skills merely to benefit those who acquire them, skills will rapidly decline to the rudimentary forms that are most easily bestowed on all comers. If, however, we believe that we teach skills in order to *keep those skills alive*, then we shall go on stretching ourselves, singling out those best able to acquire the skills in question, encouraging them to build on what they have acquired and to enhance it. This we do as much in engineering and information technology as in sport, and it is the principal argument for introducing a competitive element into education—that we thereby single out those best fitted to receive it, to enhance it, and to pass it on .

The same is true of that other form of practical knowledge—not knowledge of means, but knowledge of ends, which betokens success in action and the right feelings that engender it. Teachers who wish to impart this knowledge are not interested only in the distribution of its embryonic forms: like teachers of physics, they wish to perpetuate a communal human acquisition, that will be lost if it is never passed on. Of course, they can pass on the rudiments of virtue and sympathy in the traditional way: through the stories and maxims of a religion, and the education in manners and morals that religion facilitates. But they are aware of the vast range and abundance of human sympathy, and of its embodiment and refinement in works of art and reflection. By inducing the love of those things, they perpetuate the knowledge of the human heart. Ideal visions of the human condition, not only of what we are, but of what we are capable of, are distilled in the works of our culture. From these visions we acquire a sense of what is intrinsically worthwhile in the human condition, a recognition that our lives are not consumed in the fire of means only, but devoted also to the pursuit of intrinsic values. The reader of Wordsworth's *Prelude* learns how to animate the natural world with pure hopes of his own; the spectator of Rembrandt's *Night Watch* learns of the pride of corporations, and the benign sadness of civic life; the listener to Mozart's *Jupiter* symphony is presented with the open floodgates of human joy and creativity; the reader of Proust is led through the enchanted world of childhood and made to understand the uncanny prophecy of our later griefs which those days of joy contain. Such experiences are intrinsically valuable to us, and they are part of that inimitable knowledge of life which is the gift of culture.

In short, we should see culture as Schiller and other Enlightenment thinkers saw it: the repository of emotional knowledge, through which we can come to understand the meaning of life as an end in itself. Culture inherits from religion the "knowledge of the heart" whose essence is sympathy. But it can be passed on and enhanced, even when the religion that first engendered it has died. Indeed, in these circumstances, it is all the more important that culture be passed on, since it has become the sole communicable testimony to the higher life of mankind.

ANSWERING THE CRITIC

But this returns us to the objection mentioned at the end of the last chapter: that of the "evil aesthete" and "philistine philanthropist." Many of the most heartless people have been highly cultivated—Lenin, Hitler, Stalin, and Mao, not to speak of all those aesthetes in jackboots who commanded the camps. Many more people have been models of sympathy and virtue, relieving suffering, sacrificing comfort, courageously holding out under torture, and spreading around them kindness, justice, and goodwill, even though they have never opened a book, visited a theater or set foot in a gallery. The examples are not given merely as empirical instances: they are meant to suggest an *a priori* disconnection between "aesthetic education" and the moral life. There is no *a priori* reason why an acquaintance with culture should enliven real sympathies—indeed, every reason for believing that, by expending their tender emotions on fictions, aesthetically educated people unfit themselves for real encounters. Worse, they may be tempted to "aestheticize" the real world, putting beauty above goodness in their scheme of values, and perhaps enjoying the spectacle of suffering as part of some aesthetically appealing tableau.

There is a simple answer to that objection. Human life is conducted on a thin crust of normality, in which mutual respect maintains a genial equilibrium between people. Beneath this thin crust is the dark sea of instincts, quiescent for the most part, but sometimes erupting in a show of violence. Above it is the light-filled air of thought and imagination, into which our sympathies expand and which we people with our visions of human value. Culture is the collective practice which renews those visions and extends our sympathies into all the corners of the heart. It is the ongoing record of the life of feeling, which offers to every new generation the examples, images, and words that will teach it what to feel. But when the eruptions come it can do nothing to tame the violence. Nor can religion do anything, nor can ordinary morality. For violence breeds violence, and anger breeds anger. Good people, whether educated or uneducated, whether aesthetes or philistines, will try to bring order and decency in the midst of chaos, but bad people will always resist them, and in the worst moments of human conflict it is the bad people who prevail. Some of these bad people will be cultivated; some will be religious; all of them will be bent on a path of destruction, consulting their faith or their education only as a source of excuses, and never as an order to stop. No institution, no doctrine, no art that human beings have devised has ever been able to prevent the atrocities that occur, once the crust of normal life has broken. Why that is so is a question for the anthropologist and the geneticist; that it is so has been shown beyond doubt.

But what of the philistine philanthropist? Is he not a sure proof that morality and culture have little or nothing to do with each other, and that our educative efforts would be better spent on the first of those assets, rather than squandered (as they might be) on the second? The philistine philanthropist certainly has what people need in times of trial: the virtues that make people useful to themselves and to their fellows. But these virtues die with their possessors. Only if their memory is perpetuated in narrative, image, and song can others relish the thought of them, and learn fully to admire and to imitate what is shown to them by art. It is from our culture that we learn to understand and love the simple virtues: without Hardy's Tess, Wordsworth's Michael, Péguy's Jeanne d'Arc, and other such pictures of simplicity, we should not understand the full force of the objection that tells us that such people are admirable beyond the reach of cultured freaks like you and me.

Moreover, we should not expect from culture what religion and morality fail to provide in our times of trial. What we can expect is that culture should conserve, through whatever troubles, the message of something higher: the image of a world of human feeling which is also a proof of human worth. We pass on culture, therefore, as we pass on science and skill: not to benefit the individual, but to benefit our kind, by conserving a form of knowledge that would otherwise vanish from the world. Arnold famously defined the culture that he advocated as "the best that has been thought and said," and the phrase caught on, since it seemed to justify the enormous expenditure of energy that we devote to the task of ensuring that Shakespeare and Milton, Mozart and Bach, Bernini and Rembrandt, are as honored by our children as they are honored by us. But the phrase is only a placeholder for something more considered—for some account of what the "best" might be, in the area of thinking and saying. That is what I have tried to sketch in this chapter.

4 | The Uses of Criticism

EVEN IF IT is true that culture contains a legacy of emotional knowledge, and a record of human worth, this does not help the teacher to settle the all-important questions: which bits of culture, which works of art and literature, which cultural practices, should I place before my pupils, and how should I teach them to enjoy such things? In fact the argument of the last chapter has dropped us once again into one of the most difficult and fraught of intellectual controversies —that concerning the nature and objectivity of aesthetic values. Following previous practice, I shall cut through the knot with laughter.

INTRINSIC VALUES

Comedy is a fundamental ingredient in every serious culture, and is also an exemplary forum in which our social sentiments are put to the test. As I suggested in Chapter One, at the heart of all true amusement lies a judgment, and it is this judgment that permits us to laugh. We laugh at what falls short, what indicates smallness in the heart of grandeur or a mismatch between the ideal and the real. And in all its forms laughter is a social response: more, it is a *society-building* response. In laughing at something, even when laughing alone, I am situating myself in an imagined community of the amused: people who judge as I judge, and respond as I respond. We learn to laugh in company, and laughter seals our companionship. Hollow laughter arises from the recognition that one is alone in one's laughter, and therefore no longer truly amused.

Jokes and comedies are intrinsically interesting: we enjoy them for their own sakes and, even if it is true that they also have, or can have, a therapeutic value, that is not what interests us. Jokes and comedies exist in order to be enjoyed, and enjoyed for their intrinsic value. In short, they are aesthetic objects, and when we criticize or praise them we are engaged in expressing and defending aesthetic values. Those who think there are no aesthetic values ought to look more closely at the practice of human laughter, which is—judged from one perspective—a continuous search for them, and a repeated explosion at their discovery.

But how can we discuss such values? Does not the description of them as *intrinsic* place them beyond discussion, matters of private taste concerning which we might equally agree or agree to differ? And is that not what the old Latin tag, that *de gustibus non est disputandum* (there is no disputing tastes), was getting at? To justify an interest in something is automatically to place that thing in the realm of means— to ask, what good does it do? To answer that it is good *in itself* is simply to abandon the discussion. So, at least, it seems, and hence the title of the book by John Carey: *What Good Are The Arts?* To which Carey answers: no good at all.[19]

Suppose someone asked the question "what good are friends?" It would surely be easy to come up with a few answers, and answers that we would all endorse. Friends are a cure for loneliness; they bring help in times of trouble, cooperation in ordinary ventures, and consolation in the wake of loss. A person with friends has amplified his power, his scope, and his creative potential. A person without friends is reduced to the minimal conditions of survival.

All that suggests that a friend is *good as a means*. But suppose I approach Juliet with that thought in mind. I recognize her as a high-flyer, someone who will bring me all kinds of advantages that I could not achieve alone. I calculate all the ways in which she will benefit me, and set out to "bring her over" to my side. Is that treating her as a friend? Surely not. To treat Juliet as a friend is to value her for her *own* sake, as the particular person she is. It is to value her, to use the language of Kant, "as an end in herself." Only someone who sees other people as having intrinsic value can make friends. This does not mean that his friends will not be of instrumental value. But their instrumental value depends upon the refusal to pursue it. The use of friends is available only to those who do not seek it. Those who collect friends for utility's sake are not collecting friends: they are manipulating people.

That argument suggests that intrinsic values may also be instrumental values, but only when not treated as such. The cultivation of intrinsic values may therefore be one of the most useful of our habits. If so, there is a real question as to which things we should value for their own sakes, and how we might support and educate our judgment. Laughter again offers an illustration. When someone responds to a joke with the words "That's not funny!", it suggests a serious criticism not only of the joke, but also of the person who made it. The implication is that we are being invited to laugh at something which we should not laugh at, either because it is too serious a matter, or because laughter would be tasteless or unkind. Laughter can demean what it touches, and in rendering contemptible that which deserves our love, respect, or charity, it demeans the person who laughs. It is perfectly clear, therefore, that we can criticize jokes and point to their moral defects. And we can do this without departing from the view that jokes, if they are good at all, are good *intrinsically*, for what they are rather than what they do. The bad joke is one at which we ought not to be amused. The good joke is the one that is genuinely amusing—in other words, which both elicits amusement and justifies it. And in every case we are amused at jokes *for their own sake*, and not for their effects.

Jokes, comedies, and amusing things do, however, have beneficial effects. By laughing together we oil the wheels of society. To agree in our laughter is to agree in our judgments, and a shared joke is a much more effective way of filling a brief encounter than a shared remark about the weather, since it involves not just a belief but an evaluation. When you and I laugh together, we reveal to each other that we see the world in the same light, that we understand its shortcomings and find them bearable. We are jointly "making light of" our burdens by vicariously sharing them. Comic stories and caricatures are central to traditional cultures precisely because they prompt this response, and a civilization which cannot laugh at itself—like Islamic civilization today—is dangerous, since it lacks the principal way in which people come to terms with their own imperfection.

———

JUDGING ART

It is surely not difficult to extend that argument to art, literature, and music. These things are interesting for their own sakes. But they also confer other benefits. They create a frame of reference which permits us to communicate our states of mind. They offer consolation, amusement, enjoyment, and emotional stimulation in a thousand ways. But we do not judge them by measuring those good effects. On the contrary, we judge them on their intrinsic merits. The question before the critic is not: "does this have good or bad effects?" but "is this a proper object of interest?"

Consider the category of the obscene. It is less common today than it once was to criticize works of art as obscene. But we all understand what the criticism means. Obscenity is involved whenever the human body is placed in front of the human person, so as to eclipse the soul. This happens in the graphic display of sexual activity, and also in the graphic scenes of violence in which the body, as it were, takes over. In criticizing a work of art for its obscenity, one is implying that it is wrong to take an interest in this kind of thing. Why is it wrong? Because such an interest expresses a depersonalized attitude to the human body, an attitude that voids the human form of its moral and spiritual meaning. Of course, you may disagree with that statement, and it certainly needs more defense than I can give it here. But supposing it is true: Then it implies that there is an intrinsic and not merely instrumental defect in an obscene work of art. It is an intrinsic defect because obscenity is a quality that invites a morally suspect interest. No doubt it is an instrumental defect, too:

no doubt obscenity induces bad habits of thought, bad habits of perception, and bad habits of feeling, that infect our behavior towards others in the world of real life. But that is not what we are referring to when we criticize obscenity in art. We are referring to a defect in the work of art itself, which would be a defect even if obscenity had no discernible effects on those who were interested in it. For it is the interest itself that is wrong.

Consider now the category of the sentimental. Sentimentality, like obscenity, is habit-forming. And those to whom it appeals are frequently unaware of its principal characteristic, which is that it is a pretense. Sentimental words and gestures are forms of play-acting: pretending to noble emotions while in fact being motivated in another way. Thus real grief focuses on the object, the person lost and mourned for, while sentimental grief focuses on the subject, the person who grieves, and whose principal concern is to show his fine feelings to the world. Hence, it is a mark of sentimentality that the object becomes hazy, idealized, observed with no real concern for the truth.

Again, you may disagree with that statement. But if it is true it shows exactly why critics condemn sentimentality in art. In responding to poetry, for example, we are responding sympathetically to the expression of feeling. There are feelings with which we ought to sympathize, and from which we learn "what to feel," in the sense described in the last chapter. But there are also feelings with which we ought not to sympathize, and on whose poetic expression we should look with a critical eye. Sentimental feelings are of this kind. For they are in an important sense unreal—the result of a devious, and usually self-deceived form of play-acting. We should look on them from the distance that they strive so urgently to abolish, and regard them from that distance with suspicion. This is what Oscar Wilde had in mind when he famously said, of the unctuously written scene in which Dickens describes the death of Little Nell, that "one must have a heart of stone not to laugh at reading the death of Little Nell." That is to say, this invitation to emotion is an invitation to fake emotion, and fake emotion is the enemy of real sympathy; it is the bad habit that creates the "heart of stone."

It is possible that the commercialization of the human heart by the modern media is responsible for the hysteria with which modern traumas are greeted. But it is not such bad effects to which a critic refers, in criticizing a sentimental work of art. Sentimentality is there on the page, on the canvas, or in the notes: it is an intrinsic property of the work itself. The task of the critic is to reveal it for what it is, and to show also that a work with this defect does not justify the attention for which it clamors.

KNOWING WHAT TO FEEL

Here we should recall the argument about knowledge that I sketched in the last chapter. We "rehearse" our sympathies through our encounter with fictions, and so come to "know what to feel" in situations that we have not previously encountered. In a celebrated essay "Reality and Sincerity," published in *Scrutiny* in 1952, the critic F. R. Leavis adversely compared Emily Brontë's "Cold in the Earth" to Thomas Hardy's "After a Journey."[20] Leavis writes: 'Emily Brontë conceives a situation in order to have the satisfaction of a disciplined imaginative exercise; the satisfaction of dramatizing herself in a tragic role—an attitude, nobly impressive, of sternly controlled passionate desolation." And he contrasts Brontë's "talking *about*" emotion with Hardy's "quiet presentment of specific fact and concrete circumstance." Each poem, according to Leavis, leads us into a world and at the same time "invites a response" to that world. The response is not that of the poet, but that of the reader—though the goal of each author is to place reader and poet in sympathy. Of the first line of Hardy's poem ("Hither I come to view a voiceless ghost"), Leavis writes that "'view,' we recognize, is no insensitive perversity; it is the word compelled by the intensely realized situation, and we feel it imposing itself on Hardy (and so on us) as right and irreplaceable." The sincerity of the feeling expressed is one with the concrete nature of the situation represented—the refusal to retreat into heroic abstractions—and this sincerity compels our sympathy, as the words "imposed" on the poet impose themselves also on us.

The analysis is far from indisputable, but it guides us towards two important points. The first is that the reader's sympathy is being invited towards the emotional state conveyed by the poem, and that this sympathy may be either offered or withheld. The second is that sympathy will certainly be withheld at the first hint of insincerity, and the sign of insincerity is a vagueness, a lack of concretion, in the situation presented. Words may flow mellifluously, inviting us to endorse the poem's willed sense of tragedy, as Leavis claims to be the case in the example from Brontë. Or they may, as in the Hardy, stumble over hard and recalcitrant facts, recognizing the complexity of grief and the imperfection of those remembered feelings. In the latter case the very concretion of the imagery elicits our sympathy. We move with the poet, compelled to imagine the situation exactly as it affects him. This concretion prompts that first act of judgment which sets sympathy in motion. And when our sympathetic emotions are guided, in this way, by judg-. ment, we are "learning what to feel."

Literary devices have their own way of compelling an argument. Rhyme, rhythm, word sound, and word order may coax us forward, towards a goal which they may make it difficult to resist. In such a case—and Leavis implies that this may be true of Brontë's poem—we often find ourselves rehearsing an emotion of sympathy towards a state of mind that deserves less than wholehearted endorsement. By contrast, a poem may, through its literary devices, coax us away from a state of mind that it seems to be expressing, so permitting sympathy despite toying with desolate or dreary emotions. Consider this poem by Housman:

> I to my perils
>   Of cheat and charmer
>   Come clad in armour
>   By stars benign.
> Hope lies to mortals
>   And most believe her,
>   But man's deceiver
>   Was never mine.
>
> The thoughts of others
>   Were light and fleeting,
>   Of lovers' meeting
>   Or luck or fame.

> Mine were of trouble,
>> And mine were steady,
>> So I was ready
>>> When trouble came.

Christopher Ricks writes that "the poem says a dour cramp-ing thing, but how does it say it? With gaiety and wit."[21] The form of the poem, its dancing rhythms, and its wry reference to the unbearable sufferings of Job (quoted in the last line) all bespeak a conscious withdrawal from the posture of ado-lescent despair for which Housman is so often reproached, and—Ricks implies—this permits our sympathy, enabling us to "go along with" the feeling of the poem. The feeling is conditioned by the lightness of the poem's music, and in submitting to this music we also distance ourselves from the too-easy pathways of a callow misanthropy.

SYMPATHY AND JUDGMENT

In the examples we see two critics showing how poems can teach us "what to feel" through the exercise of sympathy. The poem "points the way to" an emotion, and invites us to sym-pathize with it. But in that very act it opens the way to judg-ment. Is the situation precisely defined? Do the language, the rhythm, the literary technique, seek to draw us on un-critically, or do they, on the contrary, invite us to see things as they are, and to offer our sympathy only on proof that it is rightly offered? These, and similar questions, all arise from an underlying thought, which is that sympathetic responses to works of art are also rehearsals of sympathies that could be applied in life. And that thought in turn suggests something important about the connection between life and literature. According to the Aristotelian idea of moral education, virtue is taught by imitation, imitation instils habits, and habits transform themselves into motives. If good literature has a moral value then it is surely because it feeds into that process, by teaching us what to feel towards the actions, characters and fates of our fellow humans. And if bad literature is to be avoided, it is likewise because it misleads us into feeling sympathy where sympathy is mistaken.

I have considered only two critical concepts—obscenity and sentimentality—and tried to show how they feature in judgments of aesthetic value. But what I have said of these two concepts can be extended to cover the other familiar tools of critical inquiry: sincerity (the "ring of truth"); tragedy; profundity; wisdom; elegance, beauty itself: all these denote intrinsic features of a work of art, and also invitations to our sympathy. Criticism aims to justify the judgments that they contain, and in doing so to distinguish the right and the wrong occasions of aesthetic interest. There is nothing paradoxical in this, nor does it go against the obvious truth that, in the last analysis, aesthetic judgment concerns the individual response to the individual work. It is as rational an inquiry as the criticism of jokes, and it shapes the great conversation which is the core of a literary culture.

Still, someone might say, even if there is this discipline at the heart of culture, we still do not know how and through what artefacts to introduce it to the young. Granted that our purpose in introducing it is not to benefit the young but to benefit culture, by appointing its future guardians, it is still the case that there is far too much culture out there, and far too little space, for want of exercise, in the only minds available to receive it. So how do we begin the task of handing things on?

5 | Teaching Culture

CHILDREN USED TO BE introduced to mathematics by learning their "times tables"—an example of the rote learning condemned by Dewey. Once the tables had been internalized, children could do simple calculations quickly, and proceed to geometry and algebra without pausing over their sums. By the age of sixteen, mathematically inclined children had mastered the basics of differential calculus and were beginning to tackle differential equations. Their first years of rote learning had in effect catalyzed a piece of inherited brain chemistry, and created the neuronal links that permit the installation of one mathematical program after another.

Things are no longer so, and mathematical competence is a dwindling asset in Western societies. One contributing factor has been the abolition of rote learning. Equally important, however, has been a peculiar intellectual fallacy, which holds that, when learning a difficult science, we should begin from the basics. Zermelo's revision of Frege and Russell showed that set-theory, rather than the logic of classes, is the foundation of mathematics, being a calculus which generates all the properties of numbers from the sparsest possible assumptions.[22] And set theory has the advantage that it can be visualized, by showing one thing lying inside or outside another. Hence arose the "new math," in which children begin from pictures representing the inclusion-relations among sets, and proceed to numbers only by abstracting them from the pictorial narrative, and never by memorizing their intrinsic relations. In effect, however, the pictures place a barrier between the children and the natural use of arithmetic in daily calculations, and all subsequent learning has been slowed by this.

THE ORDER OF TEACHING

The example teaches an important lesson. Those who understand a subject can deal with its foundations. Those who have yet to understand it must concentrate instead on its most vivid and easily memorized results. This is as true of culture as it is of mathematics, even though the knowledge involved is a knowledge of the heart and not of the head. For the literary scholar English literature arranges itself in a tree, spreading upwards from Anglo-Saxon roots, through the great trunk of Chaucer and Langland, to the fertile node of Shakespeare, after which it branches into metaphysical poetry, Jacobean drama, political philosophy, and the steady sedimentation of imaginative prose that was to become the novel. But you couldn't teach the subject according to that outline. The child will discover, in due course, that *Beowulf* and *The Seafarer* are remembered in the words of modern poetry, and this discovery will enrich the reading of all the literature that came after them. Meanwhile it is necessary to learn what is learnable.

Now it is in the nature of culture to shape itself around a canon. Readers of literature don't agree about everything, but they do agree about which works are supremely important. Everyone who enters the world of culture seeks for guidance.

But the guidance is there in the culture itself. Very soon the beginner discovers that the territory is already mapped out: that the "common pursuit" of true judgment has been at work, making roads and marking monuments. Beginning with what is moving and memorable, students uncover the links that join it to other works in the canon, and which enable them eventually to make their own mental map of the territory. All that they have to understand is that the links are made by judgment. The very faculty that is engaged in the appreciation of a work of literature is alive in the comparisons that place it in the canon.

How then should a literary education proceed? It seems to me evident that the pupil must acquire, as soon as possible, the idea of a classic—a "touchstone," as Arnold called it—in other words, a work whose significance endures across generations and provides a point of comparison for other and lesser creations. Once that idea has been acquired the pupil will have no difficulty in treating literary culture as a shared possession—a frame of reference that furthers communication among all those who acknowledge it, and which permits the steady appreciation of new works, new experiences, and new sympathies. Memorizing the classics of lyric poetry, reading aloud from the epics, performing the plays of Shakespeare: such ought to be the first steps in a literary education. For these are the steps that will permit the pupils eventually to free themselves of the teacher, and proceed along a path of their own.

That is not what we see in many schools today. Through no fault of their own, teachers are encouraged to use texts judged to be "relevant" in ways that Shakespeare and Keats are no longer relevant—texts like the poems of Maya Angelou, which supposedly engage with political realities that cannot be approached through the classics. Pupils are given J. K. Rowling's *Harry Potter* and Philip Pullman's *His Dark Materials* as their first examples of English prose, works which, for all their undeniable merits, are without clear relation to the thoughts and emotions that govern the adult world. The assumption is everywhere made that, if we are to introduce children to literature, we must use works that engage directly with the world that is theirs, or with the political realities that surround them. Of course there are routes back from the works I have mentioned to the classics: from Maya Angelou to Charlotte Brontë, whose autobiography is so close to Dr. Angelou's, from Philip Pullman to Milton, who gave us, in the battles of the heavenly powers, the scenarios for so many later epics, and from J. K. Rowling to Dickens, from whom she learned the magic of names and the love of the grotesque. But it would be better to trace the influences forward rather than backwards: to teach what is most accomplished and most imbued with real feeling, before showing how great art can filter down to a world where flights of fancy take the place of imagined states of mind.

TEACHING MUSIC

The same applies in the realm of music. It is often assumed that music, because it is not a representational art, and therefore has no conceptual or narrative content, has no moral content. It doesn't say anything, and there is nothing to appreciating it than the simple unmediated desire to listen and enjoy. Taking that line, many educators believe that there is no binding reason for teaching children to appreciate the works of Mozart, rather than to stay fixated on whatever pop group or rap star holds their current attention. In the case of literature we can make all those comparative and critical judgments that I referred to in the last chapter— arguing that this is a worthy object of sympathy and this to be avoided. In the case of music, we can do nothing except allow our students' tastes to grow and develop of their own accord.

Interestingly enough, however, it is music that dominates the few remarks about aesthetic education that we find in Plato and Aristotle. According to both thinkers the modes of music "imitate" states of mind and character, and by dancing or marching to their sound we transfer those states to ourselves.[23] Hence, it is vital to ensure that children dance or march to the right things—to the modes that inculcate virtue, rather than those that give a shape and a rhythm to vice.

That suggestion belongs to a musical culture that has vanished. But it contains an important grain of truth. In the last chapter I argued that criticism is a vital part of the understanding of literature, for the reason that literature invites us to sympathize with the emotions and characters that it presents. Through literature we can "learn what to feel," and learn in particular to discriminate among the claims made upon our sympathies. Although music is not a representational art, it shares an important feature with human life, and that is organized movement. We move with the music that we listen to, and this too is a sympathetic response, a way of shaping our inner life to fit the perceived life of another.[24] That is what Plato and Aristotle had in mind when they pointed to the educative (and diseducative) effects of music. Movement is a mark of character, and some kinds of character ought not to be objects of sympathy, not even of the wordless sympathy that is conveyed by instrumental music.

Hence many of the concepts that I mentioned in the last chapter are used spontaneously to criticize the movements of a dance: obscene, sentimental, morbid, nihilistic, narcissistic, antisocial—all those terms of criticism can be applied to dances, and by extension to the music that accompanies and provokes them. Indeed, this kind of criticism is something that we might readily engage in, for example when comparing disco music to New Orleans jazz or the Scottish Ceilidh, or techno-rock to the dances of the Spanish Renaissance. We know that dance music is an emblem and evocation of social forms and proprieties; hence, it matters how we dance, and with what kind of attitude to our partner.

Distracting the Ear

There is, however, a great difficulty in proceeding beyond that point. Young people are surrounded from the earliest age by music of an undemanding kind, designed as much to be overheard as to be listened to. And they are inoculated against its more licentious messages, which have acquired a routine and uninteresting quality that neutralizes close attention. To introduce young people to the musical culture of Western civilization—arguably one of the most lasting achievements of that civilization and one in which the greatest treasure of sentiment has been instilled—it is necessary to proceed by careful steps. In particular, they have to learn to hear the movement that lies in music itself, and which is not reducible to a regular beat in the background.

That background, however, is more than a background

of sound. It is a signal launched from the tribe. Popular songs grew from a tradition of ballad and folk music, in which an expanding repertoire of favorite tunes and devices formed the foundation of music-making. Until recently the song has been detachable from the performer—a musical entity which makes sense in itself, and which can be internalized and repeated by the listeners, should they have the skill. Of course, there is a whole branch of popular music which is improvisatory. But modern pop songs are not improvised as jazz is improvised, and do not owe their appeal to the kind of spectacular musicianship that we witness in Art Tatum, Charlie Parker, or Thelonious Monk.

Modern pop songs are meticulously put together, often by artificial means, so as to be indelibly marked with the trademark of the group. Everything is done to make them inseparable from the group. The lead singer projects *himself* and not the melody, emphasizing his particular tone, sentiment, and gesture. The melodic paucity is partly explained by this. By subtracting the melody, or reducing it to stock phrases that can be reapplied in any context, the singer draws attention to the song's one distinguishing feature, namely himself. The croaks and the groans with which he delivers it become the central features of the melodic line. The singer stands revealed exactly where the music should be. The harmony is surrendered to a process of distortion, involving much mixing and editing. It is therefore impossible to reproduce it by any means normally available. Sometimes serious doubts arise as to whether the performers made more than a minimal contribution to the recording, which owes its trademark to subsequent sound engineering, designed precisely to make it unrepeatable. The music is simultaneously ephemeralised and eternally transfixed. It is an unrepeatable moment in the life of the great machine, which, by means of the machine, can be repeated forever.

Hence, it is often impossible to sing for yourself the tunes and words of a pop-song. The best you can do is to impersonate the idol during Karaoke night at the local bar, when you have the benefit of full instrumental backing, amplification, and audience, and can briefly fit yourself into the empty groove where the sacred presence lay. This intense and cathartic experience once over, the fan must step down from the stage and reassume the burden of silence.

All this means that music, for many young people, is not really detachable from its circumstances, and not something with a life of its own. And this connects with one of the major difficulties faced by the teacher today, which is the absence of the "rite of passage" out of adolescence. The ritual transition from the virgin to the married state has all but disappeared, and with it the "lyrical" experience of sex, as a yearning for another and higher state of membership, to which the hard-won consent of society is a necessary precondition. All other rites of passage have similarly withered away, since no social institution demands them—or if it does demand them, it will be avoided as judgmental, hierarchical, or in some way oppressive. The result is an adolescent community which suffers from an accumulating deficit in the experience of membership, while resolutely turning its back on the adult world—the world in which the burden of social reproduction must be finally assumed.

Pop music, which presents the idealized adolescent as the center of a collective ceremony, is an attempt to bend music to this new condition—the condition of a stagnant crowd,

standing always on the brink of adulthood, but never passing across to it. It shows youth as the goal and fulfilment of
human life, rather than a transitional phase which must be
cast off once the business of social reproduction calls. For
many young people, therefore, it constitutes an obstacle to
the acquisition of a musical culture. It is the thing that insu-
lates them from the adult world, and all other uses of
music—singing, formation dancing, playing an instrument,
listening—arouse their suspicion.

For that very reason, however, it seems to me that musical education is of pressing importance in ensuring the survival of culture. By playing together, singing in groups or
choirs, improvising, and acquiring a repertoire of melodies,
young people prepare themselves precisely for the thing
that pop music withholds from them—the rite of passage
out of adolescence. They acquire the intimate knowledge of
a social togetherness, in which discipline and order prevail.
And they learn to discriminate between the true movement
of music, which arises from its inner life, and the fake movement of the beat, which sounds from a place beyond the
melody and beyond the realm of musical thought.

Distracting the Eye

Those remarks about musical culture resonate also in the
visual arts. Culture in all its forms is an invitation to join in
the larger society, to leave behind the teenage gang, and to
enter a world in which ancestors and their achievements
prevail. In teaching young people to appreciate the visual arts
and to create artworks of their own, you are introducing
them to a form of life in which the Master is the guide and the

authority. You are unfolding before them another and quite different form of social membership from the one that they know from their peers. You are teaching them to see the world with eyes that know what the world has meant and still can mean to the human heart. And just as pop music blocks the ears to that world, so does television screen it from the eyes. As with pop, it is not so much the content as the form that betrays all high intent. Flickering images, which hold the attention not because they mean anything but because they play on the visual nerves, are bound to short-circuit the channels through which image becomes judgment and judgment emotion. The link between image and response is directly and simply made, and as a result the response remains hooked on a world in which loud colors and offensive happenings obliterate all quieter views.

The human eye, shaped by this experience, is ill equipped for the encounter with art. Visit a modern art school and you are very unlikely to encounter those disciplines through which the masters learned the art of visual perception: life drawing, the observation of nature, still life and figurative landscapes. Even abstract art, in the tradition of Mondrian, Nicholson, Braque, and Klee, is set aside in favour of assemblages and installations, very often inspired by some dim reminiscence of Duchamp's original joke, which has long since ceased to be original. Colors are T v colors—loud, backlit, shadow-free. And the images are "in your face," flippantly transgressive in the manner of Tracy Emin's unmade bed or the "Naked Shit Pictures" of Gilbert and George. As I have argued elsewhere, much of the motive for this kind of art stems from the fear of kitsch.[25] In 1939 the critic Clement Greenberg presented the art world with a famous dilemma:

avant-garde or kitsch? No third way was offered, and "avant-garde" meant the kind of abstract expressionism that Greenberg was meanwhile carefully collecting. As a result of Greenberg's influence the art world witnessed a kind of routinization of the avant-garde, with abstract expressionist clichés replacing the figurative clichés of the Sunday painters. Routine anti-kitsch, however, has proved no more inspiring to the T V generation than figurative painting of the traditional kind. Instead many young people look for ways to celebrate the world of advertising and the moving image, and rather than shun the kitsch sentiments associated with that world they have opted, like Andy Warhol, Alan Jones, and Jeff Koons, for an open proclamation of kitsch as a legitimate form of life. This "pre-emptive kitsch," as I call it, delights in the tacky, the readymade, and the pre-assembled, using forms, colors, and images which both legitimize ignorance and laugh at it, effectively silencing the adult voice. Once again we are in the presence of the great adolescent refusal —the refusal of the rite of passage into the adult world, the rite contained in our culture.

How, in the face of this organized insolence, do teachers take their pupils to the starting point required by an artistic culture—which is the recognition of the masterpiece? The pupil must learn to recognize the power of visual art to make some fragment of the world into a permanent possession of the human consciousness—not something *out there* and *for all to see* like a Warhol Brillo box, but something *in here* and close to the heart, like a ripe old face of Rembrandt's or a Duccio angel. You learn this not by looking only, but also by applying your eye to your surroundings, and striving to draw and to paint what you see. In his great treatise *Modern*

Painters, Ruskin argued that the eye must *learn* to perceive the world, and the learning comes about through connecting the eye to the hand, and both to the soul.[26] When little Tommy and little Jennifer first shape their images of our house, they are transferring to the paper their rough inner thoughts. They are not yet looking at the world, and therefore not matching their pictures to the things that they see. The process of "making and matching" has not yet begun. But suppose Jennifer has shown, through whatever detail, that she notices things and seeks to include them. That is when teaching can begin. Which things to include and why? She has to learn the distinction between the meaningful and the meaningless detail; between the look, the color, and the light that show the essence of a thing, and the dross that obscures it. She has to learn to see the world as it is, and not as it might appear on the screen. Indeed, that might be the first step in her visual education: to take away the TV props and TV colors that veil the world from her perception.

6 | Culture Wars

EVEN IF WE can hold on to the educational disciplines advocated in the last chapter, we must still confront the sustained assault on our culture and the curriculum in which it has been embodied, an assault that comes largely from within that culture, and from those charged with transmitting it. Multiculturalists tell us that the attempt to teach Western culture as though it were the sole repository of human wisdom and achievement is not merely offensive to minorities but also doomed to failure, since the audience is no longer there to understand what we are getting at. Feminism has its own grudge against our cultural tradition, as something created largely by men and at the expence of, or even in denial of, women. For the feminist, Western culture does not merely perpetuate outmoded forms of patriarchal consciousness, but also, in its very imagery and examples, confiscates the language in which effective opposition to patriarchy can be expressed. Finally, there is the more general phenomenon, which I call the "culture of repudiation," and which has spawned a massive literature of cultural subversion throughout the postwar period, from Foucault's analysis of knowledge as the ideology of power to Richard Rorty's truth-denying pragmatism, and from Barthes's structuralist debunking of the classics to the "deconstructive virus" released into the academic air by Jacques Derrida. This culture of repudiation may present itself as "theory," in the manner of the "critical theory" of Horkheimer, Adorno, and Habermas, developing ponderous "methodologies" with which to root out the secret meaning of cultural works, to expose their ideological pretensions, and to send them packing into the past. Its aim, however, is not knowledge, but the destruction of the vessel in which unwanted knowledge has been contained.

THE CRITIQUE OF MASS CULTURE

Interestingly enough, Adorno and his associates in the Frankfurt School directed their fire not against the high culture of Western civilization—of which they considered themselves the guardians—but against the "mass culture" which warred with it, and which they insisted on seeing as a product of capitalism.[27] For Adorno, a trained musician and champion of Schoenberg, nothing was more abhorrent in the mass culture of America than its music. For him the new sounds, riddled with cliché and kitsch, were not art but ideology—the sweet pill of false consciousness which numbs the senses of the working class. The American song, Adorno argued, be it by Gershwin or Berlin, by Jerome Kern or Cole Porter, is an instrument of capitalist exploitation. It is not the consumer or the producer that is sovereign in this debased musical culture, but the "owners of the means of communication," namely the capitalist class. Under socialism, Adorno implied, all this fetishism would be blown away and the emancipated proletariat would be whistling the ideology-free music of Webern and Schoenberg in the streets.[28]

Now there is an undeniable streak of toe-curling kitsch

in the American popular music that Adorno condemned. For it is music that has escaped from the paddock of good taste into the open plains of common sentiment. This does not mean that it is morally corrupt, as Adorno thought, or that it is bent to the task of falsifying social realities. It means the opposite. This is music that incorporates the pains and joys of modern life. If it sounds so different from all the music that has gone before, then this is because modern life —the life made in America—is also different from the life that has gone before. Music has meant more in the evolution of American culture than any other art form, and from Gottschalk to Sondheim and Copland to Bernstein composers have been able to bridge the gap between the elite culture and the songs and dances of the people in a way that has no parallel in Europe. Adorno hated the music of America, because he hated the way in which American culture does not permit the highbrow and the lowbrow to grow apart. Here was a culture renewing itself without advice from the Marxist elite. Necessarily, therefore, it was doomed.

Two Cheers for America

Of course, the American song steers clear of the higher emotions, and Adorno is right to remind us of this. Where a traditional folksong like "Waley Waley" tells us of the inconsolable wretchedness of a woman betrayed, the American songbook provides us with the gentle remedies of modern life, as when Judy Garland sings of "The Man That Got Away." Such a song says goodbye to one man, by way of preparing the heart for the next, using the Big Band chorus in order to cheer the victim on. The small devices whereby

Culture Counts

ordinary people cope with ordinary disappointments are honored in this music, which seldom if ever adopts a tragic tone of voice. Its attitude to rupture is typified by Hoagy Carmichael's nostalgic "I Get Along Without You Very Well"; it uses homely images to normalize the excitement of falling in love—"If I Were a Bell" as sung by Blossom Dearie, or Irving Berlin's "I'm Putting All My Eggs in One Basket." It refuses to take a tragic attitude to unrequited desire (Rodgers and Hart's "Glad to Be Unhappy"), and it cuts down all experiences, whether of joy or sorrow, of embarrassment or humor, to a manageable size, making it clear that either they are within reach of us all or within reach of no one.

If this music invokes the higher forms of passion, therefore, it also projects them into the background. The insinuating softness with which Peggy Lee sings of "the days of wine and roses" and "the door marked nevermore" is like the candlelit supper and the folded napkins—a way of invoking the unobtainable, and imbuing it with a fairy-tale glow. This is not for you, the music says, but only because it is not for anyone. Meanwhile, let's pretend. From Frank Sinatra to Barbra Streisand, America has produced a continuous stream of singers who know exactly how to represent in their tone of voice the ordinary American heart in its ordinary heartbeat, while adding just enough exaltation to make the heart miss a beat or two. Looked at in this way, the American song has prepared mankind for the modern world of transitory attachments and temporary griefs far more effectively than has any other cultural innovation. It is one of the products of popular sentiment which has earned its place in the culture of Western civilization, by helping Westerners to understand the emotions that are coaxed from them by the democratic way of life.

THE ASSAULT ON HIGH CULTURE

Since the Frankfurters came as exiles to America, there to pour scorn on their hosts, the culture of repudiation has taken another and more homegrown form. Instead of focusing on the "mass culture" of the people, it now targets the elite culture of the universities. It is indifferent, or even vaguely laudatory, towards popular art and music, seeing them as legitimate expressions of frustration and a challenge to the old forms of highbrow knowledge. Its target is culture in the sense that I have been defending it: all those artifacts that have stood the test of time, and which are treasured by those who love them for the emotional and moral knowledge that they contain.

All teachers in the humanities have had to confront this culture of repudiation, and those who have not given in to it have wondered how to resist. Is it not perhaps, as the advocates of cultural repudiation insist, that in defending Western culture we are simply defending one culture against its successor, one social order against the one that is destined to replace it, one defunct set of values against another more suited to the postmodern world? Where is the method, after all, that would generate objective and universal truths from the study of culture? Isn't a culture a circumscribed, historical, and mortal phenomenon, which will inevitably enter a period of morbidity, as the human psyche adapts to new social conditions and new spheres of choice?

That vision of culture should not blind us to the fact that the energy behind the new approach to the humanities is largely negative. This energy is directed against the traditional curriculum far more than it is directed towards some real alternative. Indeed the alternatives are never seriously described. The idea of another order, another culture, another way of being is a pure noumenon, espoused only in order to shore up the negative judgment of Western culture. If a culture were merely a collection of beliefs to be accepted, texts to be studied, works of art to be absorbed, then it would be hard to explain the animus of the new curriculum towards the old. Once we see culture for what it is, however, this animus becomes comprehensible. A culture perpetuates the memory of a form of social membership and exalts it into something natural, unchangeable, and serene. When religious faith declines it becomes difficult for intellectuals to believe that they really belong to the same community as ordinary people. Their claims to priesthood have been exploded, and their isolation in academies sets them at an impassable distance from those whose idea of adventure is to go out and mow the lawn. Faced everywhere by customs, artifacts, and rituals that have been shorn of their old authority, the would-be priest is moved to acts of sacrilege and iconoclasm. The emergence of a culture of repudiation might therefore be a normal result of the breakdown of an old religion. What is new, however, is that the repudiation is directed not against the common people, as with Adorno, but against the very elite to which the unbelieving priest belongs.

WESTERN CULTURE AND ENLIGHTENMENT

In the face of this, we should remember that Western culture is open, by its own nature, to rational questioning. The Enlightenment made explicit what had long been implicit in the intellectual life of Europe: the belief that rational inquiry leads to objective truth. Even those Enlightenment thinkers, like Hume, who distrusted reason, and those, like Kant, who tried to circumscribe its powers, went on to rest their case in rational argument. Hume opposed the idea of a rational morality, but he justified the distinction between right and wrong in terms of a natural science of the emotions, assuming that we could discover the truth about human nature, and build on that firm foundation. Kant dismissed "pure reason" as a tissue of illusions, but elevated practical reason in the place of it, arguing for the absolute validity of the moral law. For the ensuing two hundred years, reason retained its position as the arbiter of doubt, and the foundation of objective knowledge.

The appeal to reason, the new curriculum tells us, is merely an appeal to Western culture, which has made Reason into its shibboleth, and thereby laid claim to an objectivity which no culture could possess. Moreover, by claiming Reason as its source, Western culture has concealed its ethnocentrism; it has dressed up Western ways of thinking as though they had universal force. Reason, therefore, is a lie, and by exposing the lie we reveal the oppression at the heart of Western culture. In this way the culture of repudiation involves a "taking back" of the Enlightenment: of the very thing that has enabled Western culture to admit and to endorse the possibility of worldviews other than its own, the very thing that transcribed itself into law with the American Revolution and launched Western civilization on the optimistic path which it thereafter followed.

Foucault and Discourse

A powerful tool in this new cult of darkness has been Foucault's conception of "discourse."[29] Truth, Foucault tells us, is not an absolute, which can be understood and assessed in some trans-historical way, as though through the eye of God. Truth is the child of "discourse," and as discourse changes, so does the truth contained in it. Look at any academic journal in the humanities and you will find this idea at the center of a thousand factitious debates: "Western phallocentrism and the discourse of gender"; "White supremacist discourse in the novels of Conrad"; "The discourse of exclusion: a queer perspective"; and so on. By describing arguments as "discourse" you go behind them, to the state of mind from which they spring. You no longer confront the truth or reasonableness of another's opinion, but engage directly with the social force that speaks through it. The question ceases to be "what are you saying?" and becomes, instead, "where are you speaking from?" This was Foucault's triumph, to provide a word that would enable us to reattach every thought to its context, and make the context more important than the thought.

Discourse, for Foucault, is the product of an epoch, and exists by virtue of the prevailing social "power." It is what Marx called "ideology": a collection of ideas which have no authority in themselves but which disguise and mystify the social reality. There is no more to truth than the power which finds it convenient, and by unmasking power, we disestablish truth. In any epoch there are those who refuse the prevailing discourse. These are denounced, marginalized—even incarcerated as mad.[30] Theirs is the voice of "unreason," and, for those in authority, what they utter is not truth but delirium. Foucault implies, however, that there is nothing objective in this denunciation of madness: it is no more than a device whereby the established power (the power of the bourgeois order) sustains itself in being, by safeguarding its own "truth" against the rival discourse that rejects it.

The argument can be generalized, to suggest that the traditional views of man, of the family, of sexual relations and sexual morality, have no authority beyond the power which upholds them. In his three-volume *History of Sexuality*, however, Foucault goes one step further, seeing the "problematization" of sexual pleasure as a curious form of self-limitation, with no rationale outside an irrecoverable social context. He describes his study, borrowing from Nietzsche, as a "genealogy" of morals—an explanation of beliefs which, because they have no intrinsic validity or truth, must be explained in terms of their social context, and so explained away.

For all Foucault says to the contrary, however, it might be objectively true that human society and personal fulfilment are more easily guaranteed by heterosexual marriage than by sexual transgression, and that the cultural and political capital of an epoch are more easily passed on where people devote themselves to bringing up their children in the home. Rather than being the effect of social order, the old morality could be its cause. As to which it is—cause or effect—nothing in Foucault's diagnostic method could possibly tell us. The assumption throughout is that, by tracing a belief to the power of those who uphold it, you undermine its claim to objectivity. But this assumption might be the opposite of the truth.

I believe therefore that we should take a robust response to thinkers like Foucault, and all those who wish to subvert Western culture by showing its supposedly "ideological" function.[31] We should insist on our culture as a repository of knowledge, and dismiss the Foucauldian attack on it as itself a form of ideology—a way of thinking which has not truth but power as its goal. And I believe that we should be similarly robust in response to the multiculturalists, by insisting that, if there is any meaning to the term, Western culture is already about as multicultural as a culture can get. And we should back up this view by teaching our culture as it was once taught, with proper emphasis on the classics and ancient history, on the Hebrew Bible, on medieval poetry, and on the legacy of Islamic philosophy. In other words, we should teach culture as it has been taught since the Enlightenment, in order to open the pupils' minds and feelings to the underlying oneness of the human condition.

SAID AND ORIENTALISM

Close on thirty years ago Edward Said published his seminal book *Orientalism*, in which he castigated the Western scholars who had studied and commented upon the society, art, and literature of the Middle East. He coined the term "orientalism" to denote the denigrating and patronizing attitude towards Eastern civilizations that he discerned in all Western attempts to portray them. Under Western eyes the

East has appeared, according to Said, as a world of wan indolence and vaporous intoxication, without the energy or industry enshrined in Western values, and therefore cut off from the sources of material and intellectual success. It has been portrayed as the "Other," the opaque reflecting glass in which the Western colonial intruder can see nothing save his own shining face.

Said illustrated his thesis with highly selective quotations, concerning a very narrow range of East-West encounters. And while pouring as much scorn and venom as he could on Western portrayals of the Orient, he did not trouble himself to examine any Eastern portrayals of the Occident, or to make any comparative judgments whatsoever, when it came to assessing who had been unfair to whom. Had he done so, he would have been forced to describe a literature in Arabic which is either entirely Westernized in the manner of Cairo's Naguib Mahfouz (who narrowly escaped death at the hands of a knife-wielding Islamist in 1994, and was thereafter increasingly censored), or which, having turned its back on Western culture, retreats into "the shade of the Koran," as recommended by the Muslim Brotherhood leader, Sayyid Qutb. It is cool and peaceful in the place to which Qutb invites his readers. But it is also dark. And although Qutb has not been censored by the Egyptian authorities, it is relevant to point out that he was hanged.

Said's targets were not merely living scholars like Bernard Lewis who knew the Muslim world and its culture far better than he did. He was attacking a tradition of scholarship which can fairly claim to be one of the real moral achievements of Western civilization. The orientalist scholars of the Enlightenment created or inspired works that have entered the Western patrimony, from Galland's seminal translation of the *Thousand and One Nights* of 1717 to Fitz-Gerald's *Rubaiyat of Omar Khayyam*. Of course this tradition was also an appropriation—a remaking of Islamic material from a Western perspective. But why not acknowledge this as a tribute, rather than a snub? You cannot appropriate the work of others, if you regard them as fundamentally "Other."

In fact, Eastern cultures owe a debt to their Western students. At the moment in the eighteenth century when 'Abd al-Wahhab was founding his particularly obnoxious form of Islam in the Arabian peninsula, burning books and beheading "heretics" by way of demonstrating the rightness of his views, Sir William Jones was collecting and translating all that he could find of Persian and Arabic poetry, and preparing to sail to Calcutta, where he was to serve as a judge and to pioneer the study of Indian languages and culture. Wahhabism arrived in India at the same time as Sir William, and began at once to radicalize the Muslims, initiating the cultural suicide that the good judge was doing his best to prevent. In the contrast between al-Wahhab and Sir William Jones, we witness both the creative strength of Western universalism, and the narrow bigotry that Said defended in its place.[32]

ABSOLUTIST RELATIVISM

Said typifies the culture of repudiation as it has taken root in our universities. While exhorting us to judge other cultures in their own terms, he is also asking us to judge Western culture from a point of view outside—not to set it against real alternatives, but simply to judge it adversely, as ethnocentric and even racist. The same paradoxical combination —relativism towards Western culture, absolutism in support of the undescribed alternative—can be witnessed in academic feminism. The purpose is not to extend choice but to forbid it, by putting forward an orthodoxy from which dissent will not be tolerated.

Furthermore, the criticisms offered of Western culture are really confirmations of its claim to favor. It is the universalist vision of man that makes us demand so much more of Western art and literature than we should ever demand of the art and literature of Java, Borneo, or China. It is the very attempt to embrace other cultures that makes Western art a hostage to Said's strictures—an attempt that has no parallel in the traditional art of Arabia, India, or Africa. And it is only a very narrow view of our artistic tradition that does not discover in it a multicultural approach that is far more imaginative than anything that is now taught under that name. Our culture invokes an historical community of sentiment, while celebrating universal human values. It is rooted in the Christian experience, but draws from that source a wealth of human feeling that it spreads impartially over imagined worlds. When has any Eastern culture paid to Western culture the kind of tribute that Britten paid, in *Curlew River*, to the culture of Japan, or Rudyard Kipling, in *Kim*, to the culture of India?

The Enlightenment, which set before us an ideal of objective truth, also cleared away the mist of religious doctrine. The moral conscience, cut off from religious observance, began to see itself from outside. At the same time, the belief in a universal human nature, so powerfully defended by

Shaftesbury, Hutcheson, and Hume, kept skepticism at bay. The suggestion that, in tracing the course of human sympathy, Shaftesbury and Hume were merely describing an aspect of "Western" culture, would have been regarded by their contemporaries as absurd. The "moral sciences," including the study of art and literature, were seen as part of the "common pursuit of true judgment" that I have been advocating in this book. This common pursuit occupied the great thinkers of the Victorian age who, even when they made the first ventures into sociology and anthropology, believed in the objective validity of their results, and a universal human nature that would be revealed in them.

All that has changed utterly. In place of objectivity we have only "inter-subjectivity"—in other words, consensus. Truths, meanings, facts and values are now regarded as negotiable. The curious thing, however, is that this woolly-minded subjectivism comes with a vigorous censorship. Those who put consensus in the place of truth quickly find themselves distinguishing the true from the false consensus. Thus the consensus assumed by Rorty, in his updated defence of pragmatism, rigorously excludes all conservatives, traditionalists, and reactionaries.[33] Only liberals can belong to it, just as only feminists, radicals, gay activists, and anti-authoritarians can take advantage of deconstruction, just as only the opponents of "power" can make use of Foucault's techniques of moral sabotage, and just as only "multiculturalists" can avail themselves of Said's critique of Enlightenment values. The inescapable conclusion is that subjectivity, relativity, and irrationalism are advocated not in order to let in all opinions, but precisely so as to exclude the opinions of people who believe in old authorities and objective truths.

THE NEW CENSORSHIP

Those considerations are worth bearing in mind when we consider the current state of intellectual life in Europe and America. Although there are areas like philosophy which have been for many years immune to the prevailing subjectivism, they too are beginning to succumb to it. Teachers who remain wedded to what Rorty calls "a natural and transcultural sort of rationality"—in other words, who believe that they can say something permanently and universally true about the human condition—find it increasingly difficult to appeal to students for whom negotiation has taken the place of rational argument. To point out, for example, that the cardinal virtues defended by Aristotle are as much a part of happiness for modern people as they were for ancient Greeks, is to invite incomprehension. The best modern students can manage is curiosity: that, they will acknowledge, is how they saw the matter. But we are not they.

From this state of bewildered skepticism the student may take a leap of faith. And the leap is seldom backwards into the old curriculum, the old canon, the old belief in objective standards and settled ways of life. It is a leap forward, into the world of free choice and free opinion, in which nothing has authority and nothing is objectively right or wrong. In this postmodern world there is no such thing as adverse judgment—unless it be judgment of the adverse judge. It is a playground world, in which all are equally entitled to their culture, their lifestyle, and their opinions.

And that is why, paradoxically, the postmodern curriculum is so censorious. When everything is permitted, it is vital to forbid the forbidder. All serious cultures are founded on the distinctions between right and wrong, true and false, good and bad taste, knowledge and ignorance. It was to the perpetuation of those distinctions that the humanities, in the past, were devoted. But they perpetuated them by singling out works of art, history, and philosophy that were intrinsically interesting, and the student was expected to work towards judgment, from a position of disinterested inquiry. In the culture of repudiation, judgments are not subjects of disinterested debate but inviolable orthodoxies. These orthodoxies are sometimes built into the very structure of the subject to be studied. Students of "gender studies," for example, are not free to come to any conclusion not endorsed by feminist orthodoxy, and their curriculum is organized by a political agenda, rather than an intellectual discipline. Without criticism and dispassionate inquiry, no real distinctions can be *discovered*: all are imposed from outside. And the censoriousness is in its own way a recognition of the arbitrariness of the subject—a subject that has no mental discipline internal to itself, no fund of knowledge, and nothing to communicate, apart from the foregone conclusions which it was created in order to propagate.

All that returns us to the deeply paradoxical nature of the culture of repudiation. While holding that all cultures are equal and judgment between them absurd, the new culture covertly appeals to the opposite belief. It is in the business of persuading us that Western culture, and the traditional curriculum, are racist, ethnocentric, patriarchal, and therefore beyond the pale of political acceptability. False though these accusations are, they presuppose the very universalist vision which they declare to be impossible. That universalist vision is the legacy to us of Western culture, and the reason why we should conserve that culture and pass its great teachings to the young. Western culture is our highest moral resource, in a world that has come through to modernity. It contains the knowledge what to feel, in a world where feeling is in constant danger of losing its way.

7 | Rays of Hope

THE LAST TWO chapters have recorded the difficulty of teaching culture to the young in an age of cultural degradation, and the difficulty of maintaining the status of culture in our universities, when its adversaries have full possession of the field. And my argument is likely to prompt the thought that high culture, and the cultivation of aesthetic value, are perhaps passing moments in the history of mankind. Maybe they belong to another and more innocent stage of human development. Maybe we are now emerging from that stage, into a social order in which culture is no longer regarded as a human good, no longer even understood as a distinct form of consciousness. Spengler put the point in a striking sentence which deserves pondering:

> One day the last portrait of Rembrandt and the last bar of Mozart will have ceased to be—though possibly a colored canvas and a sheet of notes may remain— because the last eye and the last ear accessible to their message will have gone.[34]

Of course, we have museums, universities, and archives devoted to maintaining the relics of our culture. But that does not guarantee that this culture will survive; for it survives, if at all, *in us*, the observers and users of these things.

And if the relics have no effect on us, what remains of their meaning? Should we not compare them to the votive offerings of some dead religion, whose last devotees have disappeared, and whose artifacts gather dust in unvisited cellars?

Those are not idle or academic questions. The greatest artists of the twentieth century returned to them time and again, not providing answers, but refining the questions until they became part of the intellectual climate. Mann, Schoenberg, Eliot, Auden, Gide, Camus—these and many more have so familiarized us with the experience of cultural decay as to create the prevailing suspicion that modern art is less a fact than a question. Can there really be any more art in an age when traditions of taste have evaporated, when the eyes and ears are saturated with stimulation, when human life is set in such rapid motion that moments of contemplation are all but nonexistent? Are we not living in the aftermath of high culture, and have we not in any case lost our faith in culture, believing that it has offered no obstacle to crime?

In response, I want to point to some rays of hope: events, movements, people who engage with Western culture in a spirit of affirmation. What I say will be inevitably anecdotal, and readers are invited to look for their own examples of hope and good works, should they wish, as I wish, to invest their energies in the perpetuation of our inheritance.

THE JUDEO-CHRISTIAN LEGACY

Underlying all the works of Western art and thought has been the legacy of Judeo-Christian monotheism, and the spirit of inquiry that has made the question of its meaning inescapable. It would be wrong to suppose that academic philosophy still belongs to that tradition of faith-based and faith-inspired thinking. But within the churches, and within the Roman Catholic Church in particular, the tradition has gone through a significant period of revival, with John Paul II conveying philosophical ideas in a clear and sincere idiom to a wide audience. And the challenge has been taken up, both here and there in universities and in the wider society. Youth movements like that founded in Italy by Father Giussani, *Communione e Liberazione*, and philosophical currents such as those set in motion by René Girard in France, by Jan Patočka in Central Europe, by Czeslaw Milosz in Poland, and by Alexander Solzhenitsyn in Russia, have given renewed animus to the idea of Western culture, and inspired many people of the younger generation to look for ways to defend it. During the dark days of communism in postwar Europe, it was culture as much as religion that kept alive the hopes and decencies of young people, and which preserved for them, in the midst of corruption, the "knowledge what to feel" that the communists dearly wished to extinguish. The work of people like Kundera, Havel, and Klíma in the Czech lands testifies to the strength of this philosophical inheritance, which for them did not depend upon religion, but purely on the ideal of Western civilization and that "care of the soul" which Plato identified as the task of the *polis*.

The interesting thing about this revival of theological and philosophical thinking is that it has, for the most part, taken place outside the university. In the communist countries, the universities were mere instruments of Party indoctrination, in which all intellectual inquiry had been extinguished, so that the transmission of culture depended upon those "underground" universities in private apartments, the story of which has been told by Barbara Day and others.[35] But it has been equally true in the free countries of Europe and North America that *engaged thinking* has moved out of the universities into private research institutions, literary circles, and small magazines—magazines like *PN Review*, which has for a quarter of a century kept the spirit of poetry alive in Britain, like *New Criterion*, which for an equal length of time has done the same for criticism in America, and like *The New Republic*, which has testified to the sincere belief in culture, as a forum of debate to which the left-wing intellectual is as much committed as his conservative opponent. The artistic and intellectual traditions of our culture are alive in the novels of Ian McEwan and Michel Houellebecq, for example, in the philosophy of Alain Finkielkraut and Luc Ferry, in the plays of Tom Stoppard and Alan Bennett, in the poetry of Charles Tomlinson, Rosanna Warren, and Ruth Padel, in the work of freelance historians like Paul Johnson and Gertrude Himmelfarb, and of freelance critics like Norman Podhoretz and James Wood.

MUSIC AND THE AVANT-GARDE

Those last names are only a few among the many that might be mentioned, as proof of the living tradition of literary thought and art in the Western world. Even in the realm of music, where aesthetic values are in permanent conflict with the background noise of modern life, the public appetite for serious works remains unabated, and modern composers are rediscovering the tonal language with which to make contact with their audience. And it is worth returning again to the current fate of music, since Western music is not only the highest achievement of our culture, but also the measure of its health in any period.

Although our musical culture has passed through a period of acute crisis, it does not seem to me that this crisis was caused either by the death of tonality or by the rise of the atonal experiments which attempted to replace it. It was caused precisely by the suspicion of tonality—a suspicion which should be seen as part of the almost universal alienation of Western intellectuals from our cultural heritage. The suspicion of tonality, like Marx's suspicion of private property, or Sartre's suspicion of the bourgeois family, or the abstractionist suspicion of figurative painting, should be seen as an act of rebellion against the only way we have of making sense of things. The root cause of our musical crisis is the same as the root cause of so many other crises during our time: namely, the rise of the intellectual class, and the culture of repudiation upon which it depends for its adversarial standpoint.

There is a tendency among ethnomusicologists to describe tonality as "Western tonality," implying that it is one idiom among many, of no universal significance. We have been encouraged to see tonality as a passing idiom, whose authority is dependent upon a vanishing musical culture. But this attitude fails to do justice to the underlying appeal of tonal harmony. The interesting thing is not that tonality arose in the West, but that its discoveries cannot be made available without being adopted—often, it is true, to the detriment of the local musical culture (as in Indian Bunjee music), but always with a greedy sense that *this* is what music needs for its enrichment.

Indeed, Western music is a symbol of Western civilization itself. It is the perfect expression of the "Faustian" spirit which Spengler identified as the prime mover of our achievements: the spirit of restless discovery, which must always go deeper into the cause and the meaning of things.[36] Not without reason did Thomas Mann choose music as the preoccupation of his modern Dr. Faustus. And in endowing his hero with the despairing thought that tonality has exhausted itself, that nothing now remains for music but a "taking back" of its greatest utterances, Mann found the perfect symbol for his belief that Western civilization had come to an end.

THE REVIVAL OF TONALITY

Announcing its own demise has been such an enduring mark of Western civilization that we should approach Mann's thesis with a measure of Faustian skepticism. But in this at least Thomas Mann was right: if we wish to gauge the health of Western civilization, then we should study its musical culture. How much remains of that tradition of listening, and with what ease and conviction are new works being added to its repertoire?

When Schoenberg first devoted his great intellect to the overthrow of tonality it was partly as a gesture of defiance towards the audiences of his day, whose habit of disrupting the concerts in which his innovative music was first performed showed how far the tacit understanding between composer and listener had already broken down. Tonality, for Schoenberg and his followers, had exhausted its potential, and its principal devices had "become banal." It was no longer possible for a composer seriously to make use of the tonal idiom, since to do so would be to compromise the demands of inner truthfulness, to play to the gallery, and to utter musical platitudes whose appeal to the uninstructed masses condemned them as unfit for spiritual consumption. In effect, the listening culture had turned against itself. By admitting too many to its precinct, the temple had been defiled. That was the master thought behind Schoenberg's innovations, and a major inspiration for Adorno, in his fervent denunciation of the American popular song.

It is tonality, however, with its unique potential to synthesize the melodic and the harmonic dimensions, that makes counterpoint and voice-leading intelligible to the ordinary musical ear, and so makes it possible for people not otherwise versed in musical theory to follow the argument of a symphony or a string quartet, and to understand the message addressed through tones to their emotions. Take away tonality, and you remove that which makes polyphony accessible to all but the experts. And an art addressed only to experts is an art detached from the culture which provides its frame of reference. It is a neurasthenic art, spectral and rarefied, cut off from the life-blood which only an audience can renew.

If all that remains to us besides pop are nightmarish "sound effects" from the modernist laboratory, then the tradition of "art" music is dead. Yet it was not dead when Adorno wrote his diatribes against the popular American music of his day: the music of Hollywood and Broadway.[37] Music still had a place in people's lives. People sang and played the popular songs, arranged them for jazz combo and marching band, incorporated them in their free improvisations at home and in church. The custom of hymn singing persisted, and provided to the musical ear an easy and faultless education in the rules of four-part harmony. Tonality was a familiar daily companion, and it is this, more than any injection of scholarship, that created the musically literate audiences that abounded in our cities. It is precisely the music that Adorno despised which opened the ears of the general public to the classical masterpieces. And it is the loss of this repertoire of half-serious music, through which the language of tonality was effortlessly internalized, that has led to the eclipse of listening.

Pop music, of the kind I criticized in Chapter five, has no survival value—far less than the music-hall songs that got up the nose of Adorno. Although it wears away the ears of those who live with it, pop cannot provide the basis for a true musical culture. It has no capacity for allusion, development, or cross-reference, no ability to free itself from the mechancial devices which are the principal source of its musical appeal. It will always be a sterile force, from which nothing proceeds apart from a habit of distraction. Eventually, like television, it will either lose its adherents, or reduce them to a zombie-like condition which will isolate them from the past of mankind. In such conditions, a new culture of listening will begin to emerge.

Ears schooled in pop seek for beat instead of rhythm, for "backing" rather than voice-led harmony, and tunes which divide into croonable phrases. Such ears are initially deaf to counterpoint, and to the real experience of tonality, as a working out in three dimensions of structural relationships. They hear in Steve Reich or Philip Glass a kind of elevated and mesmerizing version of their favorite chords, and—having no sense of structure apart from repetition—imagine this to be a paradigm of serious music. In fact the music of the minimalists is far more banal and cliché-ridden than any of the half-serious music that has gone out of circulation. Its inability to pass from accompanying figures to polyphonic order expresses its helpless fixation with the chord, as opposed to the voices which form the chord as they move through it on their melodic journeys.

The new audience also finds in the spirituality of Górecki and Tavener an accessible experience of the "higher" life of music. For theirs is serious music, with a promise of release from the alienated world of popular culture. At the same time it is composed as pop is composed, with monodic chanting over unvoiced chords. It is as though serious music must begin again, from the first hesitant steps of tonality, in order to capture the postmodern ear.

Nevertheless, there is no doubt that, thanks to composers like Górecki, Tavener, John Adams, and Michael Torke serious music is adapting to the new musical ear—the ear raised on beat, which responds to relentless ostinato far more readily than to melody or counterpoint. And the lamp of real music has been kept alight through the years of darkness: Henri Dutilleux in France, the late Gottfried von Einem in Germany, Nicholas Maw in England, and Ned Rorem and John Corigliano in the United States are among many composers of the older generation who have addressed their compositions to the cultivated ear, turning their backs on academic orthodoxies and on the culture of repudiation, in order to find new ways in which the contrapuntal tradition can speak directly to the heart. If the results are tentative, they are also real, and young people respond to them. Listening to composers of my own, somewhat younger, generation —Colin and David Matthews, Oliver Knussen, David del

Tredici, Robin Holloway—I remain convinced that the return to melody, harmony and counterpoint is now irreversible, and that the bleak noise-factories of the postmodern orchestra will soon be a thing of the past, as quaint as futurism and as empty as Dada. Perhaps nothing has been more inspiring in this connection than Anthony Payne's recent creation, from the composer's fragmentary sketches, of Elgar's Third Symphony: a brilliant and heartfelt recuperation of musical ideas and one that has helped to revitalize our musical culture.

RESTORING THE EYE

It is now common knowledge that the excesses of the art world—the vast accumulations of phenomenally expensive Brillo boxes and urinals that have filled museums around the world—are really commercial ventures, engaged in because critics have made them worthwhile, because museums subsidize them, and because there is a name to be made by commissioning and owning them. Explore the walls of ordinary civilized people, and you will find engravings, watercolors, prints, and oils with figurative meanings. It is only the culture of repudiation that insists that figurative painting should be off the curriculum in the art schools. Once we move away from the subsidized world of the museum and the art school, we find artists and their public busily engaged in the old relation between them, the one creating and the other purchasing works that please the eye and inspire the mind. The point has been well made by Roger Kimball,[38] and is brought home to us by the public-spirited work of the painter Jacob Collins, who founded the Water Street Atelier in Brooklyn, devoted to the perpetuation of the figurative tradition. Collins has now joined with other artists to start the Grand Central Academy of Art, with a classical curriculum involving three years of rigorous training in the skills (such as life drawing) required for the representation of the human spirit in its embodied form.

Those interested in visual representation will know of other such initiatives, and will have sensed the gathering movement of revulsion towards the world of readymades and installations. Rather than dwell on the future of representational art, therefore, I will say something about architecture, since this is the mirror in which a civilization views itself, as well as the most telling illustration of what the culture of repudiation has really meant in the life of the ordinary person. For three millennia Western builders looked back to their predecessors, respecting the temple architecture of the ancients, refining its language, and adapting it to the European landscape in ways that are subtly varied, entirely memorable, and, above all, humane. Then Le Corbusier burst on the scene. His plan was to demolish Paris north of the Seine and to put all the people into glass boxes. Instead of dismissing this charlatan as the dangerous madman that he clearly was, the world of architecture hailed him as a visionary, enthusiastically adopted the "new architecture" that he advocated—though it was not an architecture at all, but a recipe for hanging sheets of glass onto crates of steel—and set about to persuade the world that it was no longer necessary to learn the things that architects once knew. Thus was born the modern movement.

One by one the modernists took over the schools of architecture and extinguished in each of them the light of traditional knowledge. Students of architecture were no longer to learn about the properties of natural materials, about the grammar of moldings and ornaments, about the discipline of the orders, or the nature of light and shade. They were not to be taught how to draw façades, columns, or the fall of light on an architrave, still less how to draw the human figure. They were not to be taught how to fit buildings behind a façade—Corb didn't "do" façades—still less how to follow the line of a street or to slot a building gently among its neighbors or into the sky. The only skills permitted by the modernists were those exercised at the drawing board: designing horizontal sections that could be projected floor after floor into steel-framed towers, willfully violating the organic texture of the town in which they were to be dumped. And when the buildings landed in our cities (for the modernist propaganda had infected the planners, too) they destroyed the street-line, the skyline, and every other form of visual harmony, staring from their faceless sides with the glazed eyes of corpses. Everybody hated them, apart from the architects who had built them and the assorted megalomaniacs who had commissioned them. And even they chose to live elsewhere, usually in some Georgian pile built according to the principles that they were actively forbidding. Meanwhile, the urban working class was swept out of its genial streets to be stacked up in hygienic tower blocks, according to Corb's instructions—a brilliant idea that destroyed the city as a home, killed off the spirit of its residents, and in general released the population into the brave new world of alienation.

All those things bore witness to an important fact, namely that the decline of architecture and the degradation of our cities was not an inevitable consequence of cultural decay, but a willed gesture of repudiation. And one will can be opposed by another. Quinlan Terry was a student at London's Architectural Association in the 1960s, at the height of the modernist frenzy, when city after city was being torn apart in obedience to the utopian dogmas of Gropius, Lubetkin, and Le Corbusier. Terry was attending classes that showed how to translate insane collectivist propaganda into childish isonometric drawings. As with the art schools, real drawing, real looking, real measuring, and real moral understanding had to be learned elsewhere. Terry converted to Christianity, which taught him to question all the self-serving dogmas on which he had been raised, including the dogmas of modernism. He then set out to learn what his professors forbade, traveling to see the great monuments of Western architecture, drawing the details of country churches, studying the simple streets of not yet ruined towns, and in general equipping himself with the knowledge that an architect needs, if he is to adapt his art to its surroundings, instead of destroying the surroundings in order to draw attention to his art.

Needless to say, Terry's projects, submitted as his thesis, were failed by the examiners. In satirical spirit he submitted hubristic modernist designs instead, and was allowed to pass. He joined the firm of Raymond Erith, whose practice he inherited, at a time when there was little private business and when all public commissions went to the modernists. Terry's break came in 1984, when Haslemere Estates commissioned his designs for Richmond Riverside, which was to become one of London's most popular tourist attractions. This harmonious collection of classical buildings, rising on a knoll above the Thames, and enclosing offices, restaurants, and private dwellings, illustrates Terry's principles: to fit in to the landscape and townscape; to use an architectural language that puts a building into relation with its neighbors and with the passerby; to use natural materials and load-bearing walls, so that the building will last and weather; to respect the realities of climate and the human need for light and air; to create forms and spaces that will lend themselves to the changing purposes of their residents and which will not die, as modernist buildings usually die, with their initial function.

Richmond Riverside showed that all those traditional goals could be achieved, at a density and a cost that trump the rival plans of the modernists. As Terry has frequently pointed out, modernist buildings use materials that no one fully understands, which have a coefficient of expansion so large that all joints loosen within a few years, and which involve massive environmental damage in their production and in their inevitable disposal within a few decades as waste. Modernist buildings are ecological as well as aesthetic catastrophes: sealed environments, dependent on a constant input of energy, and subject to the "sick-building syndrome" that arises when nobody can open a window to let in a breath of fresh air.

Terry's buildings either go unmentioned in the architectural press or are subjected to dismissive polemics, focusing on their alleged nature as "pastiche." This epithet—which, if taken seriously, would condemn all serious architecture from the Parthenon down to the Houses of Parliament—has been elevated into an all-purpose critical tool, by people who are determined that no whisper from the past shall ever again be heard in our cities. Yet the popularity of Terry's buildings grows, as does their influence. Around Terry and the Luxemburg architect Léon Krier has grown a "new urbanist" movement, with several large-scale developments to its credit, including the popular residential village of Poundbury, built for the Prince of Wales in Dorset. The idea is catching on that modern patterns, style, and materials are ill understood and antipathetic towards our feelings for home. Unless used with great tact and skill, they grate against our quieter emotions, and place an obstacle before our need to settle. You can use them to compose isolated jewels like the houses of Frank Lloyd Wright, but those houses require acres of garden to set them off, and could never form the fabric of a city. The cultural inheritance embodied in the classical orders, which teach us to understand light and shade, line and volume, and the long-term impact of a building on the soul of the passerby, is therefore one that people are now learning to reclaim. And maybe this is a greater symbol of our cultural hunger even than the restoration of tonality in music or the recent return to figurative painting in the spirit of Edward Hopper or to reflective literature in the spirit of Solzhenitsyn and Günter Grass.

THE TRAGEDY OF ISLAM

The cynic will say that none of that means very much to the ordinary person, and it is true that culture remains what it has always been: the possession of an elite. But that elite is conserving and passing on a store of important knowledge. Although this knowledge may not be explicit in the heads of ordinary people, it passes, nevertheless, into their plans, their outlook, and their social adaptations. Hence, we should not be surprised that, just as the elite is showing the first tentative signs of a return to our cultural traditions, so are the forms of popular entertainment beginning to include versions, however crude, of the Western religious inheritance. The films of the Narnia stories, for example, stand beside the litanies of John Tavener and Górecki, as proof of a cultural hunger which reaches every social milieu. And the cause of this hunger is simple: people have had enough of emotional ignorance, and are beginning to be aware of its cost. Even the Harry Potter stories, godless though they are, have won an audience for their multiple allusions to old cultural icons—to the enchantment and mystery of the English public school, to the Gothic cloisters and the gothic ghosts that have always inhabited them, to the plain old-fashioned middle-class society (the "muggles") against which Harry is in rebellion and to which he inexorably belongs.

It is one of the most damaging effects of the culture of repudiation that it leads people to believe that elites stand above the mass of people, in a posture of alienation and ridicule. "Culture" appears like a weapon wielded against the ignorant, and against their moral and religious scruples. Western culture, as I have defended it in this book, is in fact the opposite of that—a sword wielded in defense of the "common man" and his values by our guardian angel, who is knowledge. And if it should be doubted that this culture is still of use to us, then study what happens to a civilization when its culture disappears. Consider Islam which, in the great days of Avicenna, al-Ghazali, and Averroës, rose to a self-consciousness and a self-mastery that filled the Islamic world with meanings and with a knowledge of the heart. What has happened to that great and disputatious culture?

Where, for example, will you find printed copies of the philosophers? In American university libraries, certainly. But not in any ordinary bookshop in the Middle East. Hafiz and Rumi are familiar in translation. But look for them in their native Iran and you will find only bowdlerized versions. You can travel all over the Muslim world and find only expurgated editions of the *Thousand and One Nights*. Novelists and poets exist, but almost everywhere under a heavy pressure of censorship. New publications in Egypt must first receive an imprimatur from the Islamic seminary of al-Azhar, and it is a good year that sees five hundred titles. There was a revival of Arabic letters in the Lebanon in the later nineteenth century, and the effect of this is still felt. But Lebanon was, at the time, a predominantly Christian country, flexing its muscles in anticipation of the Ottoman collapse. Check out the state of letters in Iran, for example, and you will be astonished to discover a country that publishes its greatest poets in censored fragments, and accords official credence to *The Protocols of the Elders of Zion*.

The same message is conveyed by the newspapers of the Arab world, which seem to be largely indifferent to the literary, philosophical, and artistic traditions of Islamic civilization, referring to them always in a wooden and distant way, as though genuflecting at an unswept shrine before proceeding to the brothel. The impression is of a mass act of cultural suicide. Of course, there are excellent native scholars of Arabic and Persian culture, but many are to be found in Western universities and those who stayed at home often live on the margins of society.

To speak of a "clash of civilizations," as Samuel Huntington famously did, is to assume that two civilizations exist.

But one of the contenders has never turned up on the battle-field. The clash that we witness is between Western secular-ism and a religion which, because it has lost its self-conscious part, can no longer relate in any stable way to those who dis-agree with it. It is precisely the loss of its culture that has permitted Islam to enter the modern world with so much death in its heart—death of others, which hides and excuses the death of self.

We in the West are more fortunate. Our culture has schooled us in the need for toleration, and prepared us for the new secular world—and it has preserved in these unlikely circumstances a precious legacy of moral knowledge. It mat-ters less that the mass of people are ignorant of this culture than that an elite is still being recruited to pass it on. Like every form of knowledge, that embodied in a culture spreads its benefits even over the ignorant, and those who make the effort to acquire that knowledge are not merely doing good to themselves: they are the saviors of their community.

THE NEED FOR THE AESTHETIC

Aesthetic values are intrinsic values, which cannot be meas-ured by price; they also prompt us to find intrinsic values in the world in which we live. At the time of the industrial rev-olution, when the thought first entered people's heads that our natural environment is vulnerable, that all on which we depend could be squandered and polluted through our mad mismanagement, there emerged an aesthetic movement which had natural beauty as its ruling cause. Burke's *Trea-tise on the Sublime and the Beautiful,* Addison's essays on the "Pleasures of the Imagination," Kant's *Critique of Judgment,* and the works of such thinkers as Price, Alison, Home, Lessing, and Rousseau, all served to place nature at the center of our aesthetic interests, and to invoke a realm of intrinsic value that was threatened by our footsteps. Now you could say that this invocation of aesthetic value, which led to the great revolution in artistic sensibility that we find in Novalis, Wordsworth, Beethoven, Schubert, Friedrich, and Constable, had a function—which was to protect the world from our predations. And that is true: the aesthetic value of nature encouraged people to renounce the hubris which says we have a right to every natural resource. But the aesthetic revolution of the eighteenth and early nineteenth centuries was effective because it opened people's eyes to intrinsic values. Natural beauty has an instrumental value, but only when valued intrinsically—only when withdrawn from the market, and fenced round with prohibitions. (Notice the parallel with friendship, as I discussed it in Chapter Four.)

Something similar is true of the aesthetic values that we discover in architectural forms, and which constrain the market in urban real estate. As the New Urbanists have shown, aesthetic values are necessary, if cities are to live: for they withdraw from the market the most important element of city life, which is the city itself, conceived as a common home and a place of public dialogue. Look at provincial American cities and you will see what I mean. American cities are planned by "zoning" laws which largely ignore the aesthetic dimension, and see the parts of the city in terms of their various economic and social functions. When aesthetic values are ignored the townscape ceases to be intrinsically lovable, the population retreats to the suburbs, there to live in mutual privacy, while the inner city decays into a merely functional structure—a structure which, by being *merely* functional, soon loses its function.

Something similar is true, too, of the fine arts of literature, painting, and music. These are replete with intrinsic values: not aesthetic values only, but the moral values which they cause to shine forth in sensory form. *King Lear* does not justify or vindicate suffering, but it leads us to see that death is not senseless, when life has striven to ennoble itself and been defeated by a fatal flaw. Criticism has aesthetic value as its subject matter. But all criticism worth the name is devoted also to revealing the moral content of works of art—the aspect that transfigures and redeems through sympathy, and which teaches us "what to feel." The moral value of art does not lie in the fact that it makes you good—maybe it has no such potential. Its moral value consists in the fact that it perpetuates the idea of moral value, by showing that *there really is such a thing.*

WHY CULTURE MATTERS

In almost every sphere we are now discouraged from offering criticism; it suffices that a work of art has an audience, that people want to look at it, to read it, to listen to it, or at any rate to overhear it. Box-office success is the received criterion of value—and while this or that person may object to pornography, gratuitous violence, to works that deliberately "do dirt on life," as D. H. Lawrence put it, they have no more right to dictate what can or cannot be made or sold or enjoyed than anybody else. Such, at any rate, is the prevailing view of things. It assumes that works of art are enjoyable, in just the way that food or drink or football or pornography are enjoyable to those who enjoy such things, and that there is no role for art in withholding our emotions from the market. On the contrary, art is another way of putting them on sale. We have entered a time when aesthetic judgments are routinely avoided. People have tastes, certainly, but these tastes are no different from their tastes in food—desires for gratification of the kind that we can witness as easily in an animal as in a rational being. What was distinctive of the aesthetic experience—namely, that it was founded in the perception of value—has dropped from the picture, and desire alone remains. If people study art at all it is often merely to explore technique, or else to "go behind" the whole tradition of artistic expression and to deconstruct its hidden political assumptions. Judgment itself—whether the judgment contained in art, or the judgment applied to it—is routinely avoided. This is part of living in a "non-judgmental," "inclusive," and maybe even "multicultural" environment.

In such an environment, aesthetic judgment is easily regarded as a threat. Nothing in the new world is to be withdrawn from the market, and if anything is forbidden absolutely it is only those things—like murder—which threaten everything. In all the areas of life where people have sought and found consolation through forbidding their desires—sex, in particular, and taste in general—the habit of judgment is now to be stamped out. There are no intrinsic values, people believe, but at best only opinions about intrinsic values. In other words, the attempt to build a realm of intrinsic value—and that is what culture really is—is regarded with suspicion. Those who demand that the attempt nevertheless be made are a threat to the social order, since they remind us that it is not an order at all, but a kind of regimented disorder where, beneath the uniform loutishness of public life, our desires compete in chaos for their satisfaction, without any public recognition that some desires deserve fulfilment while others should be suppressed.

I suspect that humanity has often entered periods like ours, in which the discipline of judgment and the pursuit of intrinsic value have declined or disappeared. When this happened in the past, however, no record was left of it, since a society without culture loses its memory and loses also the desire to immortalize itself in lasting monuments. Very soon barbarism takes over, and the society is swept from the face of the earth. What is interesting about our situation is that we have the technological means to sustain our society in being beyond the moment when it might lose all inner sense of its value, and therefore lose the ability to sustain itself from its own inherent reservoir of faith. This is a new situation, and we should ask ourselves what we might do, in these circumstances, to ensure the survival of culture. Those Irish monks who kept the lamp of learning alight during the Dark Ages of our civilization had a great advantage over us—namely, that there was no competition from loud-mouthed and amplified idiocy, that all around them was danger and destruction, and that no sooner had they found refuge than peace too stepped quietly after it to guide their thoughts, their feelings and their pens.

Nevertheless, the signs of hope that I have identified in this chapter are not isolated points of unfashionable resistance. They suggest a growing movement of revulsion against the prevailing nihilism—both the nihilism of the university, and the nihilism of the marketplace. This movement may

not succeed in placing culture once again where it belongs—
at the center of university education, and in the hearts of our
leaders. But it succeeds in showing us why culture matters,
and why the battle to conserve it should be properly fought.

Notes

1 I have tried to sort the admirable from the deplorable and the mysterious from the muddled in "Spengler's Decline of the West," in *The Philosopher on Dover Beach*, St. Augustine's Press, South Bend, Indiana (1998).

2 Kant, *The Critique of Judgment* (1790), available in various translations, which puts aesthetic judgment for the first time clearly in the center of our modern intellectual concerns.

3 See Frank Buckley, *The Morality of Laughter*, University of Michigan Press (2003), in which the nature of laughter, as a society-forming practice among moral beings, is admirably spelled out.

4 All praise nevertheless to Arthur Danto, *The Transfiguration of the Commonplace*, Cambridge Mass. (1981), a work which shows how problems of ontology are intrinsic to our normal ways of describing art.

5 John Carey, *What Good are the Arts?* London, Faber and Faber (2005).

6 J. S. Mill, *A System of Logic*, tenth edition, London, Longmans (1879), Book 1, Chapter 7, Section 4.

7 Failure to appreciate this point, I have argued, underlies the disaster of utilitarian and modernist architecture–an architecture that denies the tradition which has formed and educated the human eye. See *The Aesthetics of Architecture*, London and Princeton (1979).

8 T. S. Eliot, *On the Use of Poetry and the Use of Criticism*, London (1933).

9 Matthew Arnold, *Culture and Anarchy*, London (1869).

10 *Nicomachean Ethics* 1177b4–6, which remarks that we are busy for the sake of leisure, just as we make war for the sake of peace.

11 Friedrich von Schiller, *Letters on the Aesthetic Education of Man*, tr. E. Wilkinson and L. A. Willoughby, Oxford (1967).

12 by Mihaly Csikszentmihalyi and Robert Kubey (summarized in *Scientific American*, 23rd February 2002).

13 See Walter Burkert, *Homo Necans: The Anthropology of Ancient Greek Ritual and Myth*, tr. Peter Bing, Berkeley Cal., Univ. of California Press (1983); René Girard, *La Violence et le sacré*, Prais, Grasset (1972).

Notes

14 See Josef Pieper, *Leisure: the Basis of Culture* (*Musse und Kult*, 1948), tr. G. Malsbary, South Bend, Indiana, St. Augustine's Press (1997).

15 The Catholic recusant theory has had a striking boost recently from Patrick H. Martin and John Finnis: "The Identity of 'Anthony Rivers,'" *Recusant History* 26 (2002), pp. 39-74.

16 Gilbert Ryle, *The Concept of Mind*, London, Hutchison (1949), Chapter 2.

17 These "other kinds of trouble" include those that come about when the military ethic encounters social complexities which defy its code of honor, and its fundamental simplicity of outlook: the tragic possibilities of this are explored by Ford Madox Ford in *The Good Soldier*.

18 *Nicomachean Ethics*, 1125b.

19 John Carey, *What Good Are The Arts?*, op. cit.

20 "Reality and Sincerity" in *Selections from Scrutiny*, Cambridge, CUP (1968), vol. 2.

21 *The Force of Poetry*, Oxford (1984), p. 165.

22 Zermelo, Ernst. "Untersuchungen über die Grundlagen der Mengenlehre I." *Mathematische Annalen*, 65: 261–281 (1908). English translation, "Investigations in the foundations of set theory" in John von Heijenoort, *From Frege to Gödel*, (1967), pages 199–215. Heijenoort documents the history of one of the great achievements of our culture, for which the thinkers involved can never be sufficiently honored.

23 Plato, *The Republic*, Book 4; Aristotle, *Rhetoric*.

24 For a philosophical account of what this means, see my *Aesthetics of Music*, Oxford, OUP (1997).

25 See *Modern Culture*, 2nd edn., London, Continuum (2000), ch. 8.

26 John Ruskin, *Modern Painters*, vol. 1, London (1843).

27 See, for example, Theodor Adorno and Max Horkheimer, *Dialectic of Enlightenment*, tr. J. Cunningham, New York, Continuum (1973).

28 See Th. W. Adorno, "Über der Fetischcharakter in der Musik," in *Dissonanzen: Musik in der verwalteten Welt*, Gottingen (1956).

29 See especially his three-volume *Histoire de la sexualité*, Paris, Gallimard (1976–1984).

30 See *Folie et déraison: Histoire de la folie à l'âge classique*, Paris (1961).

Notes

31 Among whom we should count Roland Barthes (*Mythologies*, 1957), Pierre Bourdieu (*Distinction, A Social Critique of the Judgment of Taste*, tr. R. Nice, London 1984), and Terry Eagleton (*The Ideology of the Aesthetic*, Oxford 1990).

32 See the detailed account in Robert Irwin, *For Lust of Knowing: the Orientalists and their Enemies*, London, Allen Lane (2006).

33 See for example Richard Rorty, *Contingency, Irony, Solidarity*, Cambridge, CUP (1989).

34 *The Decline of the West, op. cit.*, vol. 1, p. 168.

35 See Barbara Day, *The Velvet Philosophers*, London, Claridge Press (1999).

36 Oswald Spengler, *The Decline of the West*, London (1921).

37 Theodor W. Adorno and Hans Eisler, *Komposition für den Film*, in Adorno, *Gesammelte Schriften*, Frankfurt-am-Main (1976).

38 Roger Kimball, *Art's Prospect: The Challenge of Tradition in an Age of Celebrity*, Ivan R. Dee, Chicago (2003).

INDEX

Addison, Joseph, 6, 103
Adorno, Theodor, 70–71, 74, 92, 93
Aeschylus, 24, 26
aesthetic taste, 5–6, 8–9, 14–15, 30, 87
American Revolution, viii, xii, 76
Angelou, Maya, 59–60
architecture: modernist, 96–98; "new urbanists," 98–100, 104; and zoning laws, 104–5
Aristophanes, 24
Aristotle, 24; on leisure & contemplation, 16–17, 18, 19, 21, 26; on music, 61; on virtue, 37, 55, 83
Arnold, Matthew, 14, 44, 59
art: canon of, 4, 5, 14; concept of, 8–13; Eastern, 78–80, 81; and emotions, 51–54, 106; judgment of, 5–6, 49–51, 55; and moral judgment, 14–15; and myth, 26; obscenity in, 49–50; as play, 18–19; and relativism, 10; and religion, 87–88; sentimentality in, 50–51; stone-age, 2; universalism in, 81, 84–85; *see also* visual arts
Auden, W. H., 87
Averroës, 4, 101
Avicenna, 101

Bach, Johann Sebastian, 30, 44
Barthes, Roland, 69

Baumgarten, Alexander, 6
Beethoven, Ludwig von, 104
Bennett, Alan, 89
Beowulf, 58
Berlin, Irving, 70, 72
Bernini, Gian Lorenzo, 44
Bernstein, Leonard, 71
Bible, 3, 22
Brahms, Johannes, 10
Braque, Georges, 66
British Empire, 29, 32
Britten, Benjamin, 81
Brontë, Charlotte, 60
Brontë, Emily, 51–52, 53
Burke, Edmund, 103

Camus, Albert, 87
Carey, John, 9–10, 46
Carmichael, Hoagy, 72
Charles, Prince of Wales, 100
Chaucer, Geoffrey, xii, 33–34, 58
Chinese New Year, 23
Christianity, vii, 3, 81, 87–88, 98; Communion, 23; revival in, 88
Collins, Jacob, 95–96
comedy. *See* humor
Communione e Liberazione, 88
communism, 88–89
computer science, 29; "information technology," 31–32
Conrad, Joseph, 76
Constable, John, 104
Copland, Aaron, 16, 71

Index

Corigliano, John, 94
Critique of Pure Reason (Kant),
  29–30
Curlew River (Britten), 81

Danto, Arthur, 9
Day, Barbara, 89
Dearie, Blossom, 72
Decline of the West, The (Spengler), vii–viii
deconstruction, 69, 82
del Tredici, David, 94–95
democracy, viii–ix, 73
Derrida, Jacques, 69
Dewey, John, 28, 57
Dickens, Charles, 51, 60
Diderot, Denis, 25
Duccio di Buoninsegna, 67
Duchamp, Marcel, 9, 66
Dutilleux, Henri, 94

education: aesthetic, 19, 42; "child-centered," 28, 29; and "information," 31–32; literary, 58–60; in mathematics, 29, 57–58; in music, 60–62; practical, 39–41; "relevance" of, 28–30, 59–60; and religion, 38–39; in sciences, 29, 33; in technical disciplines, 33–34; and types of knowledge, 30–37; and virtue, 37–39
Einem, Gottfried von, 94
Einstein, Albert, 30
Elgar, Edward, 95
Eliot, T. S., 14, 87
Émile (Rousseau), 28
Emin, Tracy, 66
emotions, xii, 1, 5, 13, 101; and

amusement, 7–8, 11; and art, 51–54, 106; education of, x, 18–19, 36–39, 45, 51–55, 61; Hume on, 75; and music, 71–73, 92; and sentimentality, 50–51; and sympathy, 36–37, 38, 41–42, 52–55, 61; and TV, 66
Enlightenment, xii, 3, 41, 78; on aesthetic judgment, 6; and "orientalists," 79–80; and reason, 75–76; on religion, 25, 81–82
Euripides, 24

feminism, 69, 81, 84
Ferry, Luc, 89
Finkielkraut, Alain, 89
FitzGerald, Edward, 80
Foucault, Michel, 69, 76–78, 82
Frankfurt School, 70, 73
French Revolution, viii, xii
Friedrich, Caspar David, 104
friendship, 46–47

Galland, Antoine, 80
Garland, Judy, 71
Gershwin, George, 70
Ghazali, al-, 101
Gide, André, 87
Gilbert & George, 66
Girard, René, 88
Giussani, Luigi (Father), 88
Glass, Philip, 93
Górecki, Henryk, 94, 101
Grand Central Academy of Art, 96
Grass, Günter, 100
Greek civilization, 2, 83; athletes in, 22; Dionysian festival, 23; drama, 13, 24, 26; leisure in,

16–17; philosophers in, 24, 32
Greenberg, Clement, 66–67
Gropius, Walter, 98

Habermas, Jürgen, 70
Hafiz, 25, 102
Hardy, Thomas, 43, 51–52
Harry Potter (Rowling), 60, 101
Hart, Lorenz, 72
Havel, Vaclav, 88
Herder, Johann Gottfried, 2
Himmelfarb, Gertrude, 89
His Dark Materials (Pullman), 60
History of Sexuality (Foucault), 77
Hitler, Adolf, 15, 41
Holloway, Robin, 95
Hopper, Edward, 100
Horkheimer, Max, 70
Houellebecq, Michel, 89
Housman, A. E., 53–54
Hume, David, 6, 75, 82
humor, 6–8, 10–11, 45–46, 47–48
Huntington, Samuel, 102
Hutcheson, Francis, 82

information technology, 31–32, 40
Islamic civilization, vii, 2; and censorship, 102–3; feast of 'Eid, 23; as humorless, 48; medieval, 101; and "orientalism," 79–80; Sufi poets, 25; *Thousand and One Nights*, 3, 80; Wahhabism, 80
Islamism, 79

John Paul II, Pope, 88
Johnson, Paul, 89
Jones, Alan, 67

Jones, William, Sir, 80
Joplin, Scott, 71
Judaism, 23, 87

Kant, Immanuel, 5, 6, 29–30, 47, 75, 103
Keats, John, 59
Kern, Jerome, 70
Kim (Kipling), 81
Kimball, Roger, 95
King Lear, 105
Kipling, Rudyard, 81
Klee, Paul, 66
Klíma, Ivan, 88
Knussen, Oliver, 94
Koons, Jeff, 67
Krier, Léon, 100
Kundera, Milan, 88

Langland, William, 58
Lascaux caves, 2
Latin language, 29, 30
Lawrence, D. H., 105
Leavis, F. R., 51–52, 53
Le Corbusier (Charles Édouard Jeanneret), 96–98
Lee, Peggy, 72
Lenin, V. I., 41
Lessing, G. E., 104
Lewis, Bernard, 79
literature, xiv, 51–54; canon of, 2, 3, 4, 58–59; classical, 2, 3; education in, 58–60; Greek tragedy, 18, 24, 26; and jokes, 11; Middle Eastern, 78–80; reflective, 100; sentimentality in, 51; and sympathy, 51–55, 61; universalism in, 81

Index

Lubetkin, Berthold, 98
Lucretius, 25

Mahfouz, Naguib, 79
Maimonides, Moses, 4
Mann, Thomas, 87, 91
Mao Zedong, 41
Marx, Karl, vii, viii, 76, 90
Marxism, 70–71
mathematics, 33, 57–58
Matthews, Colin, 94
Matthews, David, 94
Maw, Nicholas, 94
McEwan, Ian, 89
Mill, John Stuart, 10
Milosc, Czeslaw, 88
Milton, John, 44, 60
Mondrian, Piet, 66
Monk, Thelonious, 63
Mozart, Wolfgang Amadeus, 41, 44, 61, 86
multiculturalism, vii, 4, 78, 82
music, x, 25, 62–65, 89–95; American song, 70, 71–73, 92; and dance, 62; education in, 60–65; hymns, 92; Indian, 90; jazz, 63; Karaoke, 64; kitsch in, 70–71; minimalist, 93–94; popular, 62–65, 70–71, 92, 93; tonality, 90–95
myth, 26; Greek, 13, 22, 24

Narnia (Chronicles of), 101
New Criterion, 89
New Republic, 89
Nicholson, Ben, 66
Nietzsche, Friedrich, 25, 77
Novalis (Friedrich von Hardenberg), 104

obscenity, 49–50
Omar Khayyam, 25, 80
Orientalism (Said), 78–79

Padel, Ruth, 89
Parker, Charlie, 63
Passmore, George, 66
Passover, 23
Patočka, Jan, 88
Payne, Anthony, 95
Péguy, Charles, 43
Peter Lombard, 4
Pindar, 22
Plato: on music, 61; on myth, 24; on polis, 88
PN Review, 89
Podhoretz, Norman, 89
poetry, 89; Greek, 23; Persian & Arabic, 80, 102; and religion, 25; and sympathy, 50, 51–54; teaching of, 33–34, 58, 59
Porter, Cole, 70
postmodernism, xii, xiii, 73, 83–84; and music, 94–95
Poundbury (Dorset), 100
Price, Richard, 104
Proesch, Gilbert, 66
Protocols of the Elders of Zion, The, 102
Proust, Marcel, 41
Pullman, Philip, 60

Qutb, Sayyid, 79

reason, 33; and Enlightenment, 75–76; Kant on, 29–30, 75
Reich, Steve, 93
relativism, xi–xii, 10
religion: 22–24, 41, 44; distancing

116

Index

CULTURE COUNTS has been set in Adobe Systems' Warnock Pro, an OpenType font designed in 1997 by Robert Slimbach. Named for John Warnock, one of Adobe's co-founders, the roman was originally intended for its namesake's personal use, but was later developed into a comprehensive family of types. Although the type is based firmly in Slimbach's calligraphic work, the completed family makes abundant use of the refinements attainable via digitization. With its range of optical sizes, Warnock Pro is elegant in display settings, warm and readable at text sizes – a classical design with contemporary adaptability.

SERIES DESIGN BY CARL W. SCARBROUGH